SHELL

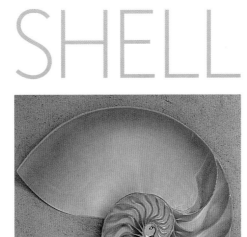

CHIC

SHELL CHIC

The ultimate guide to decorating your home with seashells

MARLENE HURLEY MARSHALL

Photographs by Sabine Vollmer von Falken

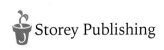

Storey Publishing

*The mission of Storey Publishing is to serve our customers by
publishing practical information that encourages
personal independence in harmony with the environment.*

Edited by Deborah Balmuth and Karen Levy
Photo styling by Marlene Hurley Marshall
Designed by Wendy Palitz and Laurie Baker
Art direction by Meredith Maker
Illustrations by Elayne Sears
Indexed by Peggy Holloway

Printed in China by Elegance
10 9 8 7

Library of Congress Cataloging-in-Publication Data

Marshall, Marlene Hurley.
  Shell chic / Marlene Hurley Marshall ; photography by
Sabine Vollmer von Falken.
    p. cm.
  Includes index.
  ISBN 978-1-58017-440-4 (alk. paper)
  1. Shellcraft. 2. Shells. I. Title.
TT862 .M37 2002   745.55—dc21

CONTENTS

DEDICATION

In memory of Michael Hurley, Laura Hurley, and Sandra Hurley Scott, who died much too young.

ACKNOWLEDGMENTS

So many talented people helped make this book happen. The artists who participated took on the challenge of creating inspired projects. For the reader, this means enjoyment of many contemporary shell pieces designed by people of very varied backgrounds. The diverse styles from such an impressive collection of artists with their own visions enhance this book.

My sincere thanks to all the artists — Lauren Clark and her daughter Catherine, Scott Clark, Janet Cooper, Michael Doherty, Quinn Doherty, Anne Fredericks, Ann Getsinger, Goz Gosselin, Robin Greeson, Pamela Hardcastle, Susie Hardcastle, Mimi Krysiak, Reginald Madison, Deborah McDowell and her daughter Sophia, Nicole Monteran, Sandy Moran, Dana and Fritz Rohn and their daughters Chloë and Phoebe, Ron Ronan, William Schade, Jim Scrimgeour, Janice Shields, John Slauson, Robin Schmitt, and Eve Zatt — for shelling out the way they did! I feel honored to know so many talented people and have enjoyed our collaboration, which has been full of good humor, challenging, and rich with inspiration.

I would like to acknowledge my friend and photographer, Sabine Vollmer von Falken, who worked long, painstaking hours with me to create the precision artistry reflected on these pages.

A special thanks to the many other people who assisted with this project: Calla Del Signore from Drygoods, Susan Kleinwald of Kleinwald Antiques, Donald McGrory of McGrory Oriental Rugs, Patrice Mullin of Mullin-Jones Antiquities, Mark Schafler and Deborah McDowell from the Helsinki Tea Company, Michael and Helen Selzer from Farshaw Books, Shirley Snyder of Snyder's Store, and Bill Webber from Verdura Cucina Rustica, all from Great Barrington, Massachusetts; Christopher Gow of Ruzzetti and Gow, Marian McEvoy from *House Beautiful* magazine, and Kathleen Moore from the American Museum of Natural History, all from New York, New York; Christine Kleineger from the Albany Museum in Albany, New York; Deborah Cunningham from the Bonnet House in Fort Lauderdale, Florida; Robert Currey of Currey and Company in Atlanta, Georgia; Allegra Graham and David Rothstein from Race Brook Lodge and Marion Miller from Vintage Linens, all from Sheffield, Massachusetts.

Many thanks to Deborah Balmuth, Karen Levy, Wendy Palitz, Laurie Baker, and Meredith Maker. for all their professional guidance throughout this project.

And last, a special thanks to my daughters, Leigh and Marlo, for their continuing love, advice, and support. A great big thanks to Quinn and Henry Doherty, for staying wet for a long photo shoot, and to their mom, Xanthi, for her patience.

PREFACE

As an artist, I love to collect beautiful things, and I find the process essential for inspiration. Seashells — exquisite bits of treasure that nature freely provides — have become one of my passions. My shell journey has been delightful and delicious, with influences and information seemingly waiting around each corner. Some lucky star (possibly a starfish) has guided the entire journey that has culminated in this book, and it has always seemed to lead me to the right people and places for information.

I have been making mosaics and designing with different materials for many years, so shells were a natural evolution for me. Photographs of ancient grottoes, with their intricate and sophisticated designs, outrageous applications, and exotic allure, often intoxicated me. I felt compelled to learn more about the history of these wonders and for years saved articles and photographs of shells. I never imagined the depth of influence that shells have had in our culture and around the world.

Finally, with a determined effort, I gathered a large number of all types of shells. Driven by visions of historical shell mosaics, I started an energetic project and was soon thrown into another fabulous obsession. I believe that working with the varied shapes, colors, and sizes of shells and adorning surfaces with these multifaceted treasures is both simple and complex. The shells themselves hold magnificent power. Even if I just pile them on a table, there seems to be no way not to create something great.

Working on this book about shells and working with the shells themselves have been sheer pleasures from the start. I was extremely fortunate from the beginning to have so many artist friends and acquaintances who took on the shell challenge and created incredibly inspired works of art. But my good luck did not stop there, because as this book developed I met other artists who have been working with shells for many years. Thus, this book presents a tremendous overview of the work of shell artists and their varied approaches to applying and designing with these fabulous beauties. The following pages are filled with inspiration of all kinds, both historical and contemporary, and shells have center stage.

shells as
ART

People are discovering that collecting and designing with shells is an interesting and romantic hobby. With the popular interest in mosaics and the desire to use natural and exotic objects in home decor, shellwork is a perfect craft. This book encompasses the styles of many artists to help you discover a broader palette and imagination for working with shells. There are many inspirational pieces, ranging from vintage to contemporary works. I hope to share my love of shells, inspire collecting, teach creative ways to use shells, and awaken a deeper sensibility for these natural works of art.

> "But there are other beaches to explore. There are more shells to find. This is only the beginning." —Anne Morrow Lindbergh, *Gift from the Sea*

Since the beginning of time, people have marveled at the beauty of shells. The popularity of collecting them has ancient origins, and it spans all cultures and classes of society. Yet different people have appreciated shells in different ways. A few shared responses include consuming their contents as a food source; trading them as currency; making jewelry and decorations from them; and using them as tools, vessels, and objects of divination. These uses were born of simple practicality and evolved into decorative sophistication, which included displaying shells in curio cabinets and using them to adorn rooms and grottoes.

In the 16th and 17th centuries, collection mania swept through Europe. At that time, collecting shells and shellwork was a hobby of the nobility and the mark of a certain status. Collectors used partitioned wooden boxes and cabinets with cotton wool–lined drawers to display and label their specimens. Dukes, earls, and barons commissioned artists to create shell rooms and grottoes in their castles and mansions.

Many aristocrats took this pastime to new heights. In the late 1500s, Hapsburg archduke Ferdinand II developed a passion for collecting shells. His castle of Ambras near Innsbruck, Austria, had four entire rooms that housed a remarkable assemblage of shells. Another pioneer was Isabella d'Este, who installed her collection of shells and shell cameos in the old Ducal Palace in Mantua, Italy, in the 1520s.

This charming assortment of vintage shellwork comes from the collection of Mullin Hones Antiques and Kleinwald Antiques, both of Great Barrington, Massachuestts. Most were made as souvenurs.

The chief credit for making shellwork one of the most popular and fashionable pastimes of the 18th century belongs to Margaret Cavendish-Bentinck, who was the Duchess of Portland, and Mary Delany. The Duchess, particularly devoted to conchology, was a leading patroness of natural history in England. Mrs. Delany was a devotee of shellwork. At her home in Ireland, she created elaborate shell surfaces, garlands of shell flowers that resembled fine carvings, and delightful shell-encrusted candelabra. Mrs. Delany also designed the grotto for the park at the Duchess of Richmond's country house, Goodwood Park, in West Sussex (see page 132).

Shell collections stored in cabinets of curiosities existed in almost every European palace and in the homes of many wealthy merchants. The Dutch, in particular, were known for their massive shell collections, because the Dutch East India Company's trade routes took them to many ports. The Dutch were among the first to take home rare cargo filled with unusual shells from little-known continents, sparking a passion for exotic curiosities. In Paris in the 1640s, the obsession with collecting shells became a large and lucrative business. Exotic treasures from the New World fascinated the wealthy, and the

TRANSIENT HOMES

Hermit crabs do not have a hard shell covering of their own, so they seek out discarded shells from mollusks. As the crabs grow larger, they abandon those homes and seek out larger ones.

passionate desire to amass large collections drew inflated prices at auctions. Ships returning from trading expeditions packed large quantities of shells, some as ballast but most to be sold for the growing decorative arts market.

The lucrative shell trade started in earnest in London in 1835. At that time, Marcus Samuel, Sr., and his wife, Abigail, opened a store near the docks of the Thames, where they sold antiques, curios, and shells. The business prospered and their son, Marcus, Jr., having grown up in the business, naturally continued it. In 1892, he launched the Shell Trading and Oil Company (the Shell Oil Company still carries the original trademark, a gold scallop shell).

The first shell collectors' association began in the Netherlands in 1720. Named "The Lovers of Neptune's Cabinet," the organization was formed to study and develop an appreciation of shells, an activity that still flourishes in many shell clubs around the world. In Japan, where shell collecting has a venerable tradition, the emperor is the foremost shell collector and owner of the nation's greatest shell collection. Hence, the rarest shell is known in Japan as the Emperor.

Today, collectors still gather shells, which represent travel to exotic shores. Scientists, architects, and artists remain inspired and charmed by treasures from the sea. And these humble, exotic creatures continue to mesmerize and entice beachcombers to pick up a shell, put it to an ear, and listen.

Where to Find Shells

Shells are found everywhere in the world — in the depths of the oceans and among coral reefs, in deserts and forests, on top of mountains, and in every type of fresh water. In fact, mammoth mounds of shells have been found in Japan, Denmark, Florida, and California with recorded measurements of up to a mile in length, half a mile in width, and 25 feet in depth. Colorful and curvaceous, shells are pieces of nature dressed in inspired form. So how do you go about acquiring these treasured gems?

Gathering shells in their natural habitat is the easiest and least expensive way to obtain a collection. Shells lying on the beach, known as beached shells, are especially abundant after a storm. Searching for them is a fun and relaxing adventure. While beachcombing, be alert and completely absorbed in your mission. Take in the total experience — the ebb and flow of the water, the wonderful free feeling of sand under your bare feet. One surprising truth, which applies to almost anything, is that if you are honestly looking, you will find plenty of shells. They will almost dance into your hands.

It also helps to know a shell's favorite hiding spots: under seaweed, clinging to rock ledges, in shallow pools of water, and on sandbars. Some are buried under the sand, so use a scoop to sift through it. Shells are constantly being washed ashore and moved around the beach, so your finds will vary from day to day. Also take note of the tides; low tide produces the best opportunity for finding shells. (Take advantage of the tide timetable available from the local chamber of commerce.) And, of course, there is the wonderful experience of diving for shells; some larger ones never make it to the beach.

You can collect other interesting objects along with shells, such as smooth pieces of beach glass, stones polished to perfection, and wonderful colored glass balls from fishing nets. Driftwood is easy to find and makes a wonderful addition to a sea motif.

The warm waters of tropical regions and ocean rivers, such as the Gulf Stream, yield the most brilliantly colored shells. South Africa's Jeffrey's Bay is the world's number-one spot for shelling (on a recent trip there, I stumbled upon a seaport town, called Mossel Bay, that is home to a wonderful shell museum). The Pacific's Sulu Islands make up the world's second-best shelling region.

A sunset evening on Sanibel Island yields a bounty of shells (top). Sandcastles are often discovered during early morning strolls on Sanibel beaches (bottom left). A beachcomber displays her preference for miniature shells for crafting (bottom right).

These necklaces made of coral, turquoise, mother-of-pearl, jet, and abalone were designed by the Santa Domingo Indians circa 1920.

SHELLS AND THE ANCIENT GREEKS

The ancient Greeks were the first to study the scientific properties of shells. Aristotle was fascinated by them and wrote many of the early textbooks about their structure and function. In fact, he assigned many of the Greek names given to shells. For instance, he named the argonaut shell in honor of Jason and the Argonauts' search for the golden fleece aboard their ship, the *Argo.* It is said that argonaut shells float on top of the water like a boat, and sailors search for them at sea as a sign of good weather.

Australia's Great Barrier Reef produces the largest shell known, the giant white clam, and many mollusks with colorful shells grow on the coral reef. Mexico has a large shell industry, too. Probably the world's largest supplier of shells is the Philippines, and exporting shells is one of the country's largest industries. In the Philippines you can find very large shells called jingle shells, also known as window shells because they are transparent and were once used to make windows and folding screens.

The mecca for shell collectors in the United States is Sanibel Island, off the west coast of Florida, where an estimated 250 shell varieties are found. Ponce de Le'on named this part of Florida the "Coast of Seashells." Sanibel, as well as its neighboring island Captiva, is considered the world's third-best shelling spot. The beaches on Sanibel and Captiva are, thanks to the play between the Gulf of Mexico's waters and the curve of the shoreline, filled with shells that wash up from faraway winter storms.

SHELLS AS ARCHITECTURE

Shells are architectural wonders. Frank Lloyd Wright, a great shell collector, studied them and used them as models for his designs, including that of the Guggenheim Museum, whose shape was inspired by a univalve. In a speech to his architecture students, Wright once said of shells, "Note the variety of their forms. And what do you build? Split-level ranch-style houses. Here in these shells we see housing of the life of the sea. It is the housing of a lower order of life, but it is a housing with exactly what we lack – inspired form. In this collection of houses, hundreds of small beings, who themselves built these houses, we see  a quality which we call invention. The beauty of variations is never finished. It is not a question of principle design. The multitudinous expression indicates what design can mean. Certainly Divinity is manifest here in these shells in their humble form of life, such greatness with such simplicity."

Cold-water shores have much to offer as well. The beaches of New Jersey and Long Island have plentiful oysters and clams. Cape Cod offers shelling on both the Atlantic and the bay shores. The coast of Maine, abundant in easily observable sea life, has plenty of shells along with other beach collectibles. As if that were not enough, there are the beautiful shores and the islands of Virginia and the Carolinas. There are myriad opportunities to search out sea treasures on the West Coast as well. Shells are found from Washington State to the Baja Peninsula. Many books provide details on where to find the best beaches, along with the types of shells to be found on each.

Be aware that, as a result of the overcollecting of live specimens, many species have become seriously depleted. Some areas now prohibit people from collecting live specimens. However, searching beaches for dead specimens does not disturb the shell animal's life cycle. You can still amass a great collection while leaving live specimens for further propagation, ensuring that your grandchildren and other future collectors will be able to enjoy them.

There are other ways to obtain shells, such as ordering them through catalogs or from dealers on the Internet (see Resources on page 150), and in some areas, buying them from retail shell shops. Ordering from dealers can be a great advantage when you are working on big projects, because you can obtain large quantities of shells that are clean and ready to use. Acquiring shells from dealers is very convenient for shell lovers who do not have time to beachcomb or may not have access to waterways or sandy shores.

A surprisingly great place to obtain shells is a local restaurant. Often, the shells from shellfish meals are simply thrown away. When you order a shellfish meal, politely ask the waiter or waitress to save the shells from your dish. Smaller restaurants that know you as a faithful customer will probably be happy to contribute to your artistic endeavor.

No matter how you come by your shells, these magical, pearly objects with their complex natural geometry are irresistible. As you create your own works of shell art, remember that you are continuing in the footsteps of collectors and artists from long ago. Happy shelling!

SHELL LIFE

The animals that live inside shells are called mollusks (though some mollusks do not have shells). The salt in a mollusk's blood is converted into calcium carbonate, which forms the shell that houses the animal. Mollusks are divided into five classes: Gastropoda (snails, conchs, cones, cowries, olives, and top shells), Polyplacophora (chitons), Pelecypoda (oysters, clams, and mussels), Scaphopoda (tusk shells), and Cephalopoda (oysters, nautiluses, and squids).

Gastropoda and Polyplacophora are univalves; they are composed of a single valve, with a shell usually in a spiral shape. About 80 percent of living mollusks belong to the univalve classes. The Pelecypoda are bivalves — pairs of hinged shells that close. In obedience to their genes, each mollusk constructs its shell to certain specifications, as accurately as though it were following a set of blueprints.

SANIBEL SHELL FAIR

Each year during the first week of March, Sanibel Island hosts the Sanibel Shell Fair. The largest exhibit of its kind in the United States, the fair provides an opportunity to obtain and learn about all kinds of shells. It also holds the country's largest and best shellwork competition. The juried show has almost 50 categories, including ones for self-collected shells, scientific competition, and shell miniatures that can be no larger than 3 inches in any direction. There is an outside tent where you can buy shells for reasonable prices. Volunteers collect the shells during the year, sort them by size and type, and donate them to raise money for the local community center. On the last day, the remaining shells are sold in large bags for three dollars each.

Attending a recent fair, I found that a warm and friendly attitude existed among everyone participating in the show. When the last few hours of the fair approached, the shell sale was announced over a loudspeaker and all the participants dropped what they were doing and rushed toward the sale. At that point, it started to pour, which made the entire affair comical, as soaking-wet shell buyers rushed to fill their three-dollar bags. And there I was, along with my sister, caught up in the frenzy to obtain shells at a discount! As the rainfall increased, the discount became even more irresistible, and I had to buy a new suitcase to carry home all the shells I purchased.

If you go to Sanibel, be sure to visit the Bailey-Matthews Shell Museum — it contains the largest shell display in the world. Raymond Burr, the well-known actor, loved and collected shells. He owned a shell-strewn island in Fiji, and he left his massive collection of Fijian cowries and cones to the museum. And don't forget that all of Florida, not just Sanibel Island, offers miles of coastline both east and west, as well as the Florida Keys, for enjoying and collecting shells.

WOMEN AS SHELL ILLUSTRATORS

Women have often been overlooked in their historical contribution to natural history. Most historical nature illustrations were attributed to men, because they were the ones who went on government surveys. One of the first prominent shell illustrators was Thomas Say's wife, Lucy Way Sistare Say. Thomas Say was a well-respected entomologist and the conservator at Philadelphia's Academy of Natural Sciences in the early 19th century.

At that time, shell collectors found it difficult to identify their finds with only the verbal descriptions that were available. Say recognized the problem and, in 1830, determined to "fix the species of our Molluscous animals, by accurate delineation in their approximate colors, so that they may be readily recognized even by those who have not extensive cabinets for comparison." Thomas Say collected and classified the shells; Lucy Say was responsible for making scientifically accurate illustrations of them.

Another female illustrator, Helen Lawson, published her drawings in books engraved by her father. Her major contribution was the mollusk illustrations for the Haldeman and Binney books, and her work was well known for its delicate beauty. However, like Lucy Say's, Helen Lawson's career existed only within the confines of family and home.

Illustrator Helen Winchester was employed at Philadelphia's Academy of Natural Sciences, where the role of women in the home was mirrored in the natural history museum. She collaborated with Henry Pilsby on a guide to North American land mollusks, photographing and illustrating shells. Even though she was some 20 years younger, her career ended pretty much when his did. There is a photograph of Pilsby and his two assistants (one being Helen Winchester) that was later published with the two women blacked out, enshrining Pilsby in solitary fame and denying the collaboration his publications required.

Things finally began to change in the 1950s, when Virginia Orr Maes, who had apprenticed with Pilsby, went on expeditions and collected and studied mollusks. She illustrated her own photographs, which added greatly to the academy's specimen collection. Shell delineation is now the province of photography, but a number of the best illustrators are still women. Some of them are research scientists who also do photography as part of their work, some are amateurs interested in documenting marine life, and some are artists whose subject is the mollusk.

PROFILE
Ann Getsinger

Ann Getsinger, who lives and works in western Massachusetts, grew up on a Connecticut dairy farm as the youngest of five children. Ann always knew that her life would revolve around art. She received numerous awards as a child and studied at the Paier School of Art in New Haven, Connecticut, and the San Francisco Art Institute.

Her subsequent training has been as a realist, and her wide range of interests and subject matter has created a direction that might be called subtle surrealism. Her fascination with shells is derived from an essential connection with nature and a lifelong affection for the coast of Maine. Ann's shell paintings are exquisite jewels that capture the mystical aspects of sea life along with a delicate sense of light and color.

Moonlit luminance

These examples of Ann Getsinger's luminescent oil on canvas paintings all measure 14 inches by 11 inches. *Scallop Shell*, on the facing page, *Two Shells in Moonlight*, at left, and *Shells with Two Pears*, below, cropped and enlarged to show detail, are from private collections.

shell
WORK

The joy of designing with shells is derived in part from creating your own works of art from these natural works of art. The curves, sculptural ridges, knobs, spines, unique patterns, surface textures, and wonderful natural colors provide endless design possibilities.

No two artists create exactly the same product, and this is especially true of artists designing with shells. As you experiment, you will develop your own methods for working with this medium. This chapter will give you the basics – the rest is up to you.

"I've got a new madness! I'm running wild for shells. The beauty of shells are as infinite as flowers." —Mary Delany, 18th-century shell artist

Before you start working with shells, it's important to consider several design principles, such as the colors, patterns, shapes, and sizes of the shells themselves, as well as the shapes, sizes, and forms of the surfaces and objects to which they will be applied.

Most shells run in a narrow color range, which leaves the artist with a rich but restricted palette of delicate pinks, soft lavenders, luminescent whites, luscious golds, and warm sands. A few shells come in stronger colors, such as oranges, dark wines, deep lavenders, and bright yellows, hues that develop in warmer waters.

Patterns are also important and should be considered in the overall design. Creating pieces with contrasting or complementary shell patterns produces different effects. Another design element to consider is which side of the shell to expose, and this choice depends on the look you favor. Each side has its own allure and interest.

Designs are also dictated by how you place shells. For instance, you can create a design by placing scallop shells in a row or arcing them in a simple fan shape. You may want to encircle a large shell or clusters of shells with bands of smaller ones. Small and medium-sized shells can frame a central motif of larger and more dramatic ones. Or large, dark shells can form a border around clusters of small, pearly shells to create an interesting contrast. However you choose to arrange your shells, keep in mind that their shapes and sizes create distinct patterns in and of themselves.

Working with three-dimensional objects presents a few challenges that also affect your design. The kind of surface or object you plan to cover will influence your selection of shell colors, shapes, and sizes. Separate your

This vintage lamp owned by Snyder's Antiques of Great Barrington, Massachusetts, stands 6 feet tall and features a shade made of sea fans.

An early Victorian mirror, designed with a scalloped border using miniature shells, is similar in style to that of sailor's valentines made during an earlier period. Victorian shellwork was no doubt influenced by the romantic nature of the pieces brought from the Caribbean by American seamen.

shells by types and sizes so you can see how much you have of each one and plan your design accordingly. Do you prefer a light touch or a saturated surface? Consider how far out you want the shells to protrude from the object and how much you want them to nestle into the surface. Also, consider whether the shell is too large or too small in proportion to the object it will cover.

Purchased Shells

When you purchase shells from a dealer, they will arrive clean and ready to use. However, one small, select type of bivalve comes with the two sides glued together. The best way to separate them is to boil them in water for about 20 minutes. If a few remain stuck together, insert a small, sharp implement into the seam.

VICTORIAN BOUQUETS

Victorian artists who crafted flowers out of shells had materials quite different from those available to shell flower designers today. Waterproof materials were unknown in the 19th century. The flowers' leaves were made of cotton or silk, and the stalks were fashioned from uncoated wire. Shell bouquets were always protected by round glass domes, which is why many of them are preserved in such good condition today.

1

A SAMPLING OF SHELLS

1. Pearl oyster
2. Cockle
3. Conch
4. Chambered nautilus
5. Jingle
6. Spirula
7. Top left: Nerite; Others: Moon snail
8. Atlantic Bay scallop
9. Top: Babylonia; Center: Miter;
   Left and right: Cut shell
10. Beach glass
11. Sea biscuit
12. Top: Conch; Left: Spined whelk;
    Bottom: Murex; Right: Drillia
13. Top and center left: Lightning
    whelk; Bottom left: Conch;
    Right: Tulip
14. Wing oyster
15. Abalone
16. Center: Candy cane snail;
    Left/right: Yellow land snail

2

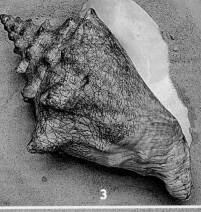

3

4

5

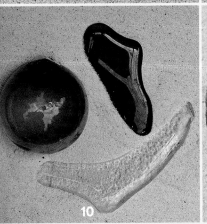

6

7

8

9

10

11

12

13

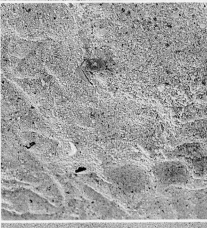

14

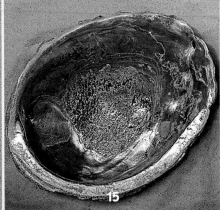

15

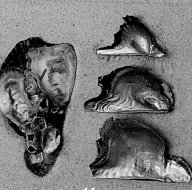

16

17

18

19

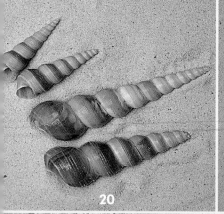

20

21

22

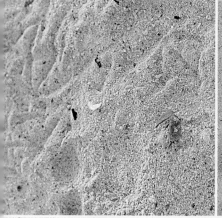

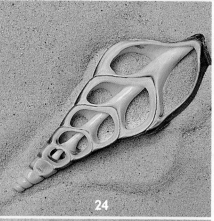

23

24

25

17. Irish flat scallop
18. Cone
19. Beach rock
20. Auger
21. Top: Donkey's ear;
    Bottom: Mule's ear
22. Olive
23. Calico scallop
24. Center-cut cerith
25. Rose cup
26. Starfish
27. Florida spiny jewel box
28. Polished turban
29. Flat tree oyster
30. Cat's eye
31. Mussel
32. Beach coral

26

27

28

29

30

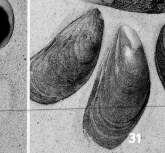

31

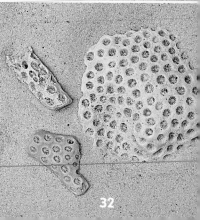

32

33

34

33. End-cut strombus
34. Sea urchin spine
35. Sand dollar
36. Cockle
37. Polished surf clam
38. Top right: Princess
    marginella; Others: Cowrie
39. Sunrise tellin
40. Worm-shell
41. Polished top shell
42. Blue limpet
43. Limpet
44. Sliced abalone
45. Dosinia

35

36

37

38

39

40

41

42

43

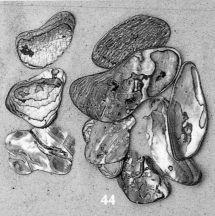

44

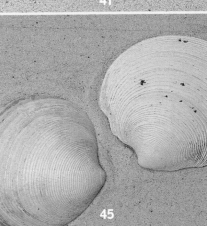

45

shellwork **19**

This shell-framed mirror and drop-front desk with starfish medallion were designed for Ruzetti & Gow's Manhattan showroom.

Cleaning Found Shells

The shells you find on beaches and along waterways need to be cleaned thoroughly before you can use them in any project. First, use a stiff-bristled brush to clean off the sand and foreign matter stuck to the shells. Soak the shells for a few hours in a solution of 1 part water to 1 part household bleach, then rinse them in clean water. If they have a strong fishy smell, soak them in a solution of ½ cup of baking soda to 1 quart of water. Set them out to dry on newspaper in the fresh air, if possible, to ensure a complete airing out. To give cleaned shells the luster that they had at the shore, rub them with baby oil or mineral oil.

If your shells are badly encrusted with foreign matter, you can soak them in muriatic acid. If you use this product, you must protect your skin and wear gloves. In a hard plastic bucket, mix 1 cup of muriatic acid with 3 cups of water. Let the shells soak for a few seconds, then use a long-handled utensil to remove them from the solution. If any stubborn substance remains, dip them for a few more seconds. Then rinse them in clean water and set them on newspaper to dry.

Preparing the Base Surface

It's important to examine the object you wish to cover and make sure it is sturdy and in good shape. If you plan to cover a wall space, make sure it is structurally sound. If the surface will be outdoors or exposed to moisture, use an exterior-strength adhesive. You do not want all of your fine work to come undone because the object you selected was in poor condition or the glue you used was the wrong type.

Types of Glue

There are many materials used to apply shells to surfaces. The type of glue you use depends on the extent to which your shell-encrusted object will be subjected to water. If exposure to water will be constant, use a strong, water-resistant glue. The weight of the shell also determines the type of glue used to hold it in place. The variety and types of glues available are much too numerous to mention here. I will cover the types I have used and those employed by the other artists in this book. Do your research, think about your project's needs, and obtain information from craft stores, other crafters, and suppliers (see Resources on page 150).

BOND 527

This multipurpose cement is popular with shell artists and can be found in craft stores. A very durable, flexible, and fast-drying product, Bond 527 can be used on china, glass, metal, leather, wood, paper, and most plastics. It is extremely strong and dries crystal clear.

CEMENT

This can be purchased at a hardware store and is a good material to use if your shell project will be outside and subjected to many types of weather, especially winter conditions. Mix the cement, spread it on the project surface, and let it set for about 10 minutes. Then place the shells in the cement. The thickness of the cement also presents some design possibilities. If you want the shells to be deeply embedded, apply a thick layer of cement to the surface of the project. The deeper the shells are set, the stronger the surface will be.

CG-9000

My personal favorite, CG-9000 is an adhesive and sealant. It is called cool glue, because it comes with a gun but is not heated. Unlike regular hot glues, CG-9000 produces glue joints that are shock-resistant and flexible. It is very thick, has excellent bonding qualities, dries in about 24 hours, and has no odor. The glue and gun can be ordered online or through the FPC Surebonder Corporation catalog (see Resources on page 150).

CLEAR SILICONE SEALANT

Available at hardware stores for interior and exterior use, silicone sealant is used with a ratchet gun made especially for tubes of adhesives, caulks, and sealants. The gun enables you to control the amount of glue that is released, which helps you pace your work and apply only as much glue as you need at a particular moment. Because the sealant is clear, you don't have to worry about seeing it between the shells, but you do need to make sure that the color and condition of the surface under the shells will be acceptable when it shows through the clear glue.

Another way to design with shells is demonstrated in Lauren Clark's box. Here, blue limpets form a distinctive wave pattern amid a sea of tiny pearl uboniums. (See the project on page 32).

In addition, silicone sealant is water resistant and has a very strong grip. It dries in 12 to 24 hours, so you will have enough time to rearrange your design if you change your mind. The glue has a strong noxious odor, so make sure you have adequate ventilation if you use it. There are so many types of adhesives in tubes that it may be a little overwhelming to select one for your project, so ask questions at the hardware store and explain your needs; a well-informed clerk can help you make the right selection.

GOOP

An industrial-strength household adhesive and sealant, Goop can be used on any type of surface, including glass, metal, rubber, wood, tile, and concrete. It goes on clear and dries within 10 minutes. Because of its short drying time, I use it when I want to hold a large shell in place while I continue with the rest of my work. However, I don't recommend it for use on outdoor projects.

HOT GLUE GUN

This product is popular with a lot of crafters; it dries in seconds and can be used on most surfaces. The guns and glue come in various sizes and are available at craft and hardware stores. Hot glue creates messy glue strings and

objects can snap off when the project is moved, as the glue is sensitive to temperature changes. I use a hot glue gun only for indoor projects, quick fixes, and solid surfaces.

PC-7

A two-part epoxy glue, PC-7 is very thick and sticky and dries in about 24 hours. Since it is waterproof, it can be used on outdoor projects. It has a dark gray color when dry. PC-7 can be purchased at hardware stores.

PLASTER OF PARIS

Setting shells in wet plaster creates a beautiful effect. Plaster cannot tolerate moisture in large amounts, but it has its place in certain projects. The drying time is about 30 to 35 minutes, so work only a small surface to allow ample time to arrange your design. Both hardware and craft stores carry this product.

SKILLET GLUE

Available at craft stores and online from FPC Surebonder Corporation, skillet glue is heated in a glue pot, which keeps it at an even temperature. A glue pot allows you to use tiny amounts of glue as necessary and without the strings that a hot glue gun produces.

TACKY GLUE

A popular craft glue that has a thick consistency and does not run, tacky glue can be found in craft and hobby stores.

THIN-SET CEMENT

This type of cement is used to set tile floors. I once used it for an outdoor shell-covered plant stand; it creates a strong bond and stops rust from bleeding through. Thin-set cement comes in white or gray, or you can add pigments to it. This allows you to tailor the background color to match or contrast with the tone of the shells. Thin-set cement dries in about 8 hours and is great for outdoor projects. Clean the cement off the shells immediately, because it stains and is hard to remove once dry.

The folding screen at right, designed by Marian McEvoy, is one of a matching pair in her Manhattan apartment. The glass jars on the bottom shelf contain some of her shell collection.

mother-of-PEARL

Pearls are among the earliest precious gems. The penchant for decorating objects, the body, clothing, and furnishings with them has a long and rich history. In the Americas, native peoples lavishly decked their canoes in pearls. Incan kings wore sandals and ceremonial garments adorned with pearls. The native peoples of Peru and Ecuador dove for pearls, then decorated their pottery with depictions of those diving scenes. Excavations of ancient Peruvian graves have revealed copious strings of pearls, containers filled with pearls, and pearl-decorated clothing.

"The sea . . . it is nothing but love and emotion; it is the 'Living Infinite.'"

—Jules Verne, *Twenty Thousand Leagues under the Sea*

ot to be outdone by pearls, mother-of-pearl also has a long history of decorative uses. This iridescent substance is composed chiefly of calcium carbonate, as well as other organic matter. The mantle encircling a mollusk's body deposits the material in thin, overlapping layers inside the shell. The interference of reflected light waves creates the luminescent play of colors. Mother-of-pearl, also called nacre, is obtained from the inner layer of nautilus, paper nautilus, turbo, abalone, trocha, giant snail, and mussels; pearl oysters produce the largest quantities.

Native Americans made jewelry boxes from mother-of-pearl. The British Museum in London houses a pillar from the temple at Al-Ubaid in southern Iraq that dates from about 2500 B.C.E. It is covered with intricate inlayed mother-of-pearl in the shapes of triangles and diamonds. Other cultures have used inlaid mother-of-pearl to decorate objects ranging from tribal masks to elegant furniture.

This chapter introduces you to working with mother-of-pearl. Keep in mind that you can adapt these projects and ideas to your own style. Have fun, relax, and trust your imagination to transform ordinary objects into dreamy, shimmering designs.

A clock encased in a polished mother-of-pearl turban shell is displayed alongside a vintage sailor's anchor and a miniature shell box.

Accessories Ensemble

The hat, shoes, and pocketbook ensemble shown above was designed by Janet Cooper. A jewelry designer and teacher, Janet transforms pieces of fabric, buttons, and vintage dolls into vignettes of mystery and magic (see more of her work on page 114). She is presently deconstructing vintage purses to turn them into dolls. Janet is an obsessive collector of wonderful things to use in her work.

Pink and blue cultured pearls and miniature shells were the inspiration for this ensemble. Janet used Goop to affix the shells and pearls to the shoes and the bag.

The shells on the hat were sewn onto the fabric through tiny drilled holes. The same types and colors of shells and pearls were used on all the items to create the sense of a matching set.

Vase with Pearls

I decorated the vase with pearls shown at right. Browsing at a flea market, I found the vase and fell in love with the iridescent copper color of the glaze. I created a swag shape with the pearls and allowed some of the wonderful copper color to remain exposed.

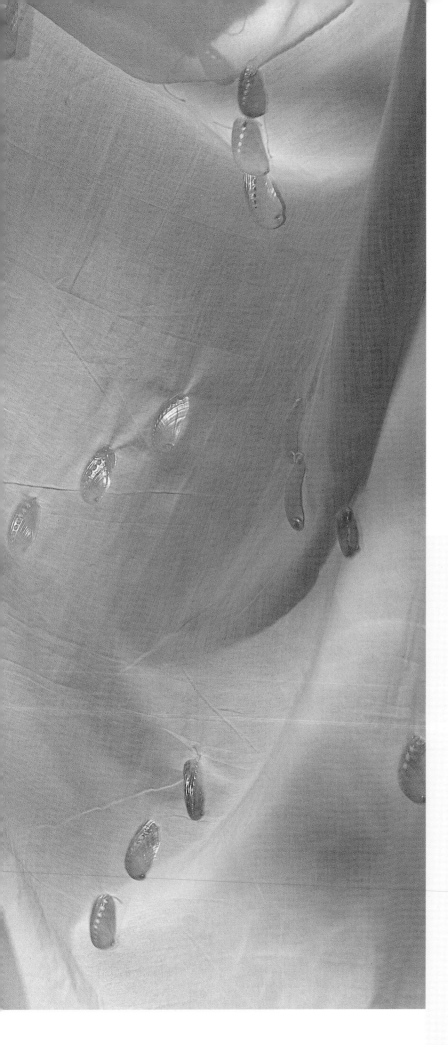

Fabric with Shells

Susie Hardcastle, who lives and works in western Massachusetts, is a fabric designer, a quilter, and an artist of many talents. Her silk scarves are painted with exotic and colorful fantasy flowers. Her quilts are exquisite pieces of art with hand-painted fabrics sewn together in unexpected ways and graced with wonderful hand stitching in many colors. There seems to be nothing that Susie cannot create.

For this project, Susie searched for the perfect fabric in stores and catalogs and finally settled on cotton gauze, because light can filter through it yet it is strong enough to hold shells. The shells, called donkey's ears, have a very delicate pearly surface with tiny swirls on one end. They are lightweight and have natural holes, which makes it easy to sew them onto fabric. A string of freshwater pearls provides a tieback for the curtain.

A PEARL OF AN EXHIBITION

The American Museum of Natural History in New York City mounted a wide-ranging exhibit titled "Pearls" that opened in the fall of 2001 and traveled to the Field Museum in Chicago. The exhibit explored the subject of the pearl — the only precious stone made by a living creature — in biology, anthropology, sociology, ecology, chemistry, history, and art. The most comprehensive display ever mounted on the subject, the exhibit included everything from 90-million-year-old fossil pearls to live pearl oysters, from a lavish pearl brooch designed by Paulding Farnham for Tiffany & Co. to costumes from the Pearlies of England. Neil H. Landman, the exhibit's chief curator and a specialist in fossil mollusks, explained, "For many years I veered between art history and natural history. Both, you see, are based on beautiful objects that tell stories."

shell-encrusted box Designed by Lauren Clark

Lauren Clark makes marbleized paper and teaches this ancient art to others. She is co-owner of Tokonoma Gallery & Framing Studio in Housatonic, Massachusetts. This project allowed her to use some of her paper designs with a new medium.

Materials

Round vintage cheese box or any box

Ruler or compass

Graph paper

Scissors

Sheet of mounting adhesive

Large sheet of marbleized paper
(see Resources on page 150)

Pencil

Goop

Mini strawberry top shells

Small blue limpet shells

Small white pearl shells

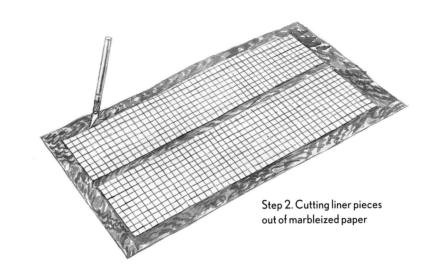

Step 2. Cutting liner pieces
out of marbleized paper

1. To line the inside and the out-side of the box, measure its height, width, and circumference, transfer the measurements to graph paper, and cut out the pieces.

2. Attach the sheet of mounting adhesive to the back of the sheet of marbleized paper. Use the graph-paper templates to cut liner pieces out of it. To make an interesting but more complicated design, find the center of the lid with a ruler or a compass; cut the paper into 12 equal triangles. Rearrange the order of the pieces and glue them to the lid. Or, for a simpler pattern, cut out a circle, using the box lid as a tem-plate. Be sure to add ¼ to ½ inch to the inside (bottom) circle; the edge will then be covered when you line the inside wall with paper.

3. Peel the paper off the mounting adhesive and affix the marbleized paper in this order:

    A. Inside bottom

    B. Inside side wall

    C. Outside side wall

    D. Top of the cover

Step 3. Affixing marbleized paper to box

4. Starting at the top of the box, use a pencil to draw a spiral pattern from the center. Then glue the mini strawberry top shells in a circular pattern, spiraling out to the edge of the box. Allow the paper to show through the rows of shells.

5. Draw a wave pattern on the cover and sides of the box and glue small blue limpet shells to follow the pattern. Again, let the mar-bleized paper show through the rows of shells to create an interest-ing background.

6. To complete the spiral on the lid, glue small white pearl shells in the spaces between the mini straw-berry tops. To complete the waves on the sides of the box, glue small white pearl shells in the spaces between the blue limpets. The white pearl shells help define the two designs.

Step 5. Gluing blue limpets
in a wave pattern

hand mirror with buttons

Designed by Marlene Hurley Marshall

An old tortoiseshell mirror I found at a flea market inspired this project, but any hand mirror will do. The mother-of-pearl buttons were also a flea market find, but new mother-of-pearl buttons can be used as well. The finish on the back of the mirror was old and scratched, which made it a perfect candidate for a new surface. The result is a lacy appearance brought to life with an iridescent shimmer. The simple instructions for assembling this mirror begin on the next page.

BUTTON TREASURES

Before the development of plastic, most buttons were made of mother-of-pearl. Shells were steam-heated, flattened, and cut into button blanks in tones of pink, blue, and smoky gray. They were so durable that they usually outlived the garments. Fortunately, people often saved buttons from old clothing. Today, you can find tins and glass containers full of these wonderful treasures at rummage sales and flea markets.

hand mirror with buttons

Materials

Bond 527

Mother-of-pearl buttons in a multitude of shapes, colors, and sizes

Vintage hand mirror or any hand mirror

Tweezers

1. Using Bond 527, affix small star-shaped mother-of-pearl buttons to the mirror's handle.

2. Glue a large button in the center of the mirror back, then glue a slightly smaller button on top, then an even smaller one, then finish the stack with a tiny baby-sized button. This gives the design some depth. Maintain a sense of balance as you place two additional button stacks on each side of the centerpiece, and then cover all but the outer edge of the mirror with buttons.

3. Encircle the mirror edge with the same star-shaped buttons used on the handle. Use tweezers to fill any gaps with miniature baby buttons.

Step 2. Gluing stacks of buttons symmetrically on mirror back

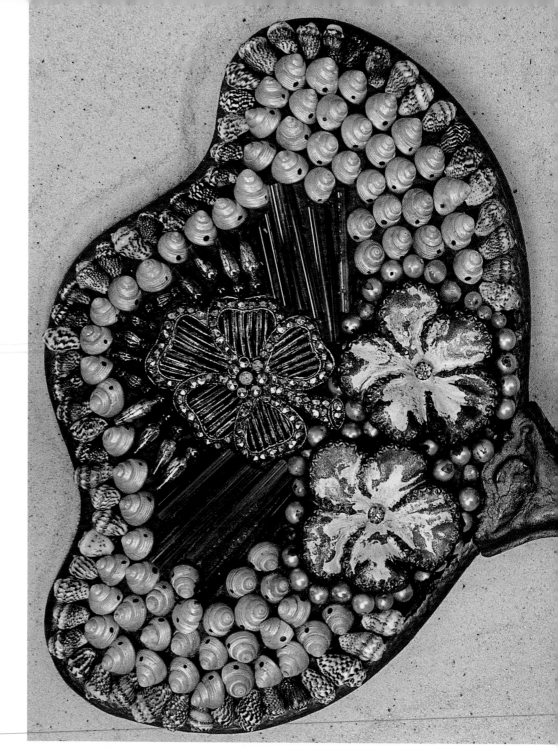

Mirror with Shells and Pearls

This hand mirror with shells and pearls was designed by Robin Greeson. Robin restores antique textiles and deals in Oriental rugs and American Indian jewelry. She has a wonderful eye for quality textiles and restores these elegant vintage gems with delicate skill. She and her husband, Donald, operate McGrory's Oriental Rugs in Great Barrington, Massachusetts. Because Robin enjoys going to flea markets and finding objects to decorate, this project was a natural for her. Robin found this metal mirror at a flea market, but any hand mirror will do. She used costume jewelry, glass beads, and pearls, along with tiny mother-of-pearl shells. Her glue of choice is PC-7.

A vintage octagonal box inlaid with mother-of-pearl is a fine example of this intricate and meticulous art form. The delicate pattern of birds and trees is completely symmetrical and reflects light in a kaleidoscope of shimmery hues.

Chair Covered with Fabric and Shells

This chair was designed by Mimi Krysiak, an extremely talented upholsterer who produces furnishings of the highest quality. Her sense of design and attention to fine detail give her work an outstanding distinction. This new creative challenge allowed her imaginative spirit to blossom.

Mimi used beige satin fabric to cover an old chair, then made channeled indentations with beige yarn to create a scalloped look to the upholstery. She used a hot glue gun to apply shells as tassels to the trim and painted the legs a deep sea blue–green to complete the fantasy.

PEARLY KINGS & QUEENS

The London tradition of the Pearly Kings and Queens was started in 1875 by a young orphaned boy named Henry Croft. From the age of 13, Henry worked as a street sweeper at the Somerstown Market. There he was drawn to a group of traders called the Coastal Mongers, who decorated their trousers and jackets with pearl buttons. Inspired by the flashy merchants, Henry covered an entire outfit with pearl buttons to attract attention and raise money for his orphanage. Before long, he was successful.

To expand his efforts, Henry asked his friends to do fund-raising too, thus beginning the tradition of the Pearlies. Eventually, every London borough had a Pearly King and Queen, who were involved in charitable work and wore the traditional button-covered uniform. The Pearlies are highly respected, and their reign is passed down through the generations.

A Pearly King's jacket reflects a proud tradition and graces the wall of a collector's home.

designs for
the
HOME

Shells are a fashionable decorative element for any room, and they have inspired a range of stylish furnishings as well. One talented designer, Marian McEvoy, used shells as a dominant theme in her chic Manhattan apartment shown at left. Another designer, Kaffe Fassett, created for his book *Glorious Interiors* an entire shell-motif room, with shell-themed rugs, paintings, and fabrics. The inspirations for these designers admittedly come from the European shell grottoes of a much earlier period. Yet the beauty of shells is that you can create atmospheres from the playful to the elegant to the exotic.

PROFILE
Marian McEvoy

The former editor in chief of *House Beautiful* and *Elle Décor* magazine, Marian McEvoy is known for her tremendous sense of style in fashion and interior design. She has written articles on the history of shell collecting and shell applications. When she was 19, she visited the studio of Tony Duquette, a famous designer who is known for having no fear of materials. His use of shells, coral, and roots in interior decor awakened in Marian an awareness of the sumptuousness of nature. When she moved to Europe in 1974, she visited the grottoes at Woburn Abbey and Goodwood Park, which deepened her interest in shellwork. Now an avid collector, she has covered her New York apartment with gorgeous speci- mens so that she can be surrounded by nature at home.

Grand scale
One of two fabulous back-to-back shell-encrusted fireplaces graces Marian's living room, shown on the facing page. She painted each shell white, then applied them with hot glue to the black background. The ceiling has a marvelous shell border, with shell medallions enhancing the design at regular intervals.

Study in black and white
A delightful shell-covered elephant candleholder, shown at left, sits in a place of honor on Marian's fabulous mantelpiece. In the bedroom, shown above, a backdrop of screens features shells placed in the center of a stark, criss-crossed design. The shell-topped mirror reflects another piece of shell art, and many shell-laden furnishings also adorn the room.

"Shell furniture was always meant to be fanciful and humorous — it is not intended to knit brows."

—George Read, former curator of English furniture at Sotheby's

child's claw-foot bathtub

Designed by Marlene Hurley Marshall

This miniature bathtub is just delightful, and I thought it would be enchanting for a child to take a bath in a tub saturated with lovely shells. This size tub will, of course, be hard to find, but the same treatment with shells would be grand on a regular-sized claw-foot tub. Be sure to use an adhesive that can be subjected to a lot of moisture.

child's claw-foot bathtub

Materials

Miniature claw-foot bathtub

White rustproof paint

Ratchet gun

Tube of clear silicone adhesive

Shells in a wide range of shapes, sizes, and colors

White beach glass

Pearl-shaped beads

Cotton batting

1. Wash the tub and touch up any scratches or rust spots with white rustproof paint.

2. Experiment with laying out different types of shells and designs. (I feel it is a good idea to just jump in to a project and follow your intuition, rather than overplan a design. I make decisions as I work, always giving myself permission to change my mind.)

3. If you are working on a freestanding miniature tub, lay it on its side so you can work more easily. If you are working on an installed tub, you will need to get comfortable on the floor. Using a ratchet gun, apply the clear silcone adhesive to the area you plan to work on, then wait about an hour for it to become sticky; this helps hold the shells in place. If your shells still slide around, use a small dab or two of hot glue to hold them until the stronger adhesive dries. The drying time is about 12 hours, which gives you some time to change your design, if necessary.

4. To achieve the design shown, place the scallop shells in the center of the tub's side with the small, straight edges parallel to each other, leaving 1–2 inches of space for the pearly turban types. Then glue a large band of bulla shells around the

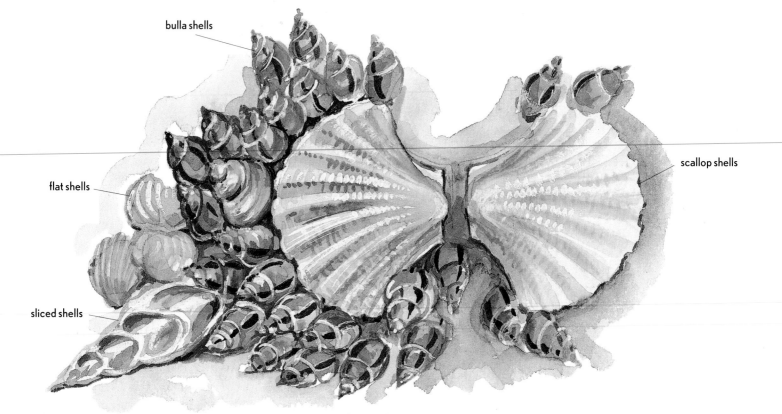

bulla shells

flat shells

sliced shells

scallop shells

Layout of center motif

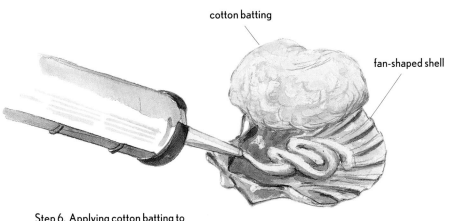

cotton batting

fan-shaped shell

Step 6. Applying cotton batting to create a flat bottom for shell

scallop shells (see illustration on facing page). Use flat and sliced shells to create an outer border with smaller, darker scallop shells rising in a straight line from the legs. Attach two large white scallops on the tub's feet, then fill in the open spaces with several types of smaller shells. Use white beach glass to fill the large spaces between the rows of scallop shells, then fill in any remaining spaces with miniature turban shells. Last, apply artificial pearl-shaped beads randomly to give the tub a bit of dazzle and whimsy.

5. If you are working on a free-standing tub, let the glue set for at least 12 hours before you turn the tub over to work on the other side. You can repeat the same design on the other side or create an entirely different one.

6. For the ends of the tub, I used donkey ear shells, which are pearly and lightweight. At the middle of the curve, I used two fan-shaped shells joined together to create a heart. Because the heart was curved outward, I filled it with cotton batting, then glued it on. You can use this technique for any shells that need a flatter area for attaching to rounded surfaces. If any shells are rather heavy, prop them up with a stick until they set.

7. When everything was completely dry and the plumbing was connected, I put a plug in the drain and plunked in my two grandsons for a fun-filled bath experience!

A ROMANCE WITH SHELLS

Shells have engaged and inspired people throughout the ages, providing a source of artistic pursuit for those who have been bitten by the shell bug.

For example, Gertrude Jekyll, born in London in 1843, was well known in the United States and Europe as a painter and landscape gardener. She lived well into her 90s and was accomplished in many handcrafts.

As her eyesight failed, she was forced to give up many pursuits. Shells, with their raised surfaces and textures, were a perfect material for Gertrude to work with, and she turned her artistry to designing shell flowers. Her fanciful creations took the place of the gardening and painting of her younger days.

Another woman who turned to shells in her later years was Louise Travers, who found herself widowed and retired in the early 1960s. With a box full of shells she had collected over the years and the inspiration of her small assemblage of sailor's valentines, she started creating decoupages of shell flowers set in shadow boxes. After seeing her first piece, her daughters each wanted one. The requests multiplied, and Louise soon found herself in production.

Drawn to ancient lore and legends about shells, shell forms in art and architecture, and the astonishing history of mollusks, Louise wrote *The Romance of Shells,* a charming story about the surprising journey her life took after she was introduced to shells.

Shell Frame

This shell frame was designed by Robin Schmitt, the co-owner of Tokonoma Gallery & Framing Studio in Housatonic, Massachusetts. She is a master framer with a discerning eye for quality craftsmanship, which is reflected in the glasswork, jewelry, and paintings in her shop.

For this project, Robin first made the larger, flat frame and then created a smaller, flanged frame to sit on top of it, giving a sense of depth. As a finishing touch, a cut nautilus was glued to mat board and placed in the center of the frame.

Shell Mirror

Susie Hardcastle designed the frame for this mirror, which she found at a tag sale. It wasn't very old, but it had a large, solid wooden frame and a nicely beveled mirror. She affixed the shells with Liquid Nails and a ratchet gun. Several large scallop shells were placed on top of the mirror frame to extend the height of the crown.

Large Mirror with Shells

The dazzling mirror shown above started out as a fabric-covered backboard for a twin bed. Reginald Madison stripped off the fabric, glued a mirror to the center with silicone, and smothered the perimeter in enormous shells, coral, starfish, and crushed bottles obtained from the local dump. A talented painter and sculptor, Reginald has exquisite taste for stunning objets d'art. He grew up in Chicago, started painting at a very young age, and received a fellowship to study art in Germany. His talents spill over into everything he touches, and he presently deals in 20th-century paintings.

Mirror with Small Shells

Anne Fredericks purchased the 1920s Russian frame, shown at right, at a flea market and used shells from her collection, which she has been amassing for more than 30 years. This project was a departure from her usual work in the Renaissance technique of water gilding, a form of gold-leaf gilding in which a skin of thinly beaten gold-leaf is applied to surfaces. All of her pieces are gilded and contain images of and messages about the environment. She lectures about endangered plants and animals, drawing on plant mythology and the role of artists as "keepers of the flame," the repository for society's conscience.

Flower Vase with Shells

Robin Greeson designed the flower vase with shells, shown below. For the base, she used a chunk of marble, which she found in her yard slightly covered in moss. She bought a metal vase at a flower shop and glued it to the marble using PC-7 two-part epoxy glue. The basic layout of shells is echoed on all four sides.

A whimsical vintage shell lamp, made from a large conch shell inserted into a giant starfish, is just one of the many shell-related items in William Schade's "happy room" (see page 56).

Shell Lampshade

The lampshade at left was designed by Deborah McDowell. Using a hot glue gun, Deborah covered a tattered old lampshade with shells to create a dramatic beaded valance with a lacy appearance. An old iron lamp base perfectly complements the elongated shade.

An artist and a writer, Deborah resides on a small farm with her two young daughters. She is the owner of the Helsinki Café and Club in Great Barrington, Massachusetts, where she has created a wonderful Bohemian atmosphere with colors, textures, furnishings, fabulous food, and exciting music.

folding screen

Designed by Marlene Hurley Marshall

This project was inspired by the refined and elegant shellwork patterns in the dining room at Woburn Abbey (for more on Woburn Abbey, see page 132). I found this screen at a tag sale and replaced the top three panels, which were fabric, with wood. You can create your own design on the folding screen or duplicate the one shown by following the instructions below.

Materials

Folding screen with wood panels

Blue-green milk paint

3" paintbrush

Pencil and ruler

Selection of shells (I used blue limpet shells, tiny cut turban shells, pink flower shells, donkey's ears, tiny pearl turbans, and Irish flat scallops)

Silicone glue and ratchet gun

Old paintbrush

Spray adhesive

Clear acrylic spray paint

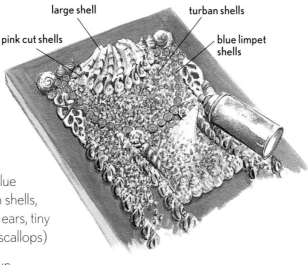

Step 3. Applying adhesive spray

1. Lay the screen out flat on a large worktable or floor and paint it.

2. Use a pencil and a ruler to find and mark the center of each panel. Lay out the shells to plan a design.

3. Using silicone glue, attach a large shell at the top center of each panel. Run a bib-shaped bead of silicone under the lower left edge of the large shell and tuck pink cut shells into the glue. Attach a semicircle of blue limpet shells below, as shown in illustration. Paint silicone inside the bib shape with an old paintbrush and sprinkle on miniature turban shells to create a shell-encrusted surface. To ensure that all of the small bits of shells stay on the surface, spray the area with adhesive after all the shells are attached.

4. Squeeze two lines of silicone about 2 inches apart on each side of each panel. Push cut bulla shells (or any medium-sized shells) into the silicone to create the columns on both sides. Paint silicone inside the lines and sprinkle miniature turban shells over the entire surface inside the lines.

5. Place an Irish flat shell in the center of each panel. Create a box design in the lower center of each panel and fill it with shells, then make a trim of shells around the outside. Attach pearly donkey's ear shells at the base of each panel.

6. Spray the entire surface with a clear acrylic coat to protect the shells and the painted surface.

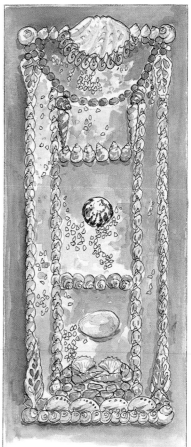

Basic panel layout

Playful drama

An enormous clamshell was adapted to create a working sink, as shown at top. Above, a dazzling shell chandelier hangs in their grotto bathroom.

PROFILE
William Schade

William Schade is an artistic genius of multiple talents who works in almost every medium. A professor of art at The Sage Colleges in Syracuse, New York, and the recipient of many awards and grants, William has a long list of museum and gallery exhibitions. Yet one does not need to know about all the awards and museums, because the man himself is the epitome of art. His home is a wild and wonderful world that speaks volumes about who he is and what he is about. From the moment I walked into William's elegant and playful environment, I knew that I was about to be taken on a delightful journey.

A tour of his home in Williamstown, Massachusetts, reveals numerous shell designs by William and his partner, Tom Branchick. They collect the majority of their shells in France and then happily drag them home in a suitcase through customs. In their amazing shell-encrusted bathroom, every surface is completely smothered with shells, and a large clamshell functions as a sink. The ceiling features a border of enormous snail shells and a central medallion that flows into a hanging shell light fixture. The pièce de résistance is a shell mosaic portrait of Neptune that faces you straight on. William says that arriving guests, having been informed about the room prior to their visit, seem to use the bathroom almost immediately!

I must say a few words about the "happy room" on the second floor of their house. This room is at once a sacred and an out-of-control shrine of wonder, a sanctuary of obsession and sheer abandonment to the creative spirit. Stepping into this room filled to the brim with vintage and contemporary shell designs is an over-the-top visual experience akin to taking a spiritual bath in the essence of exuberance.

Outrageous applications

This view greets all who enter the extraordinary grotto bathroom, shown at left. A close-up view illustrates the detail in the portrait of Neptune, shown above, which faces the commode.

PROFILE
Christopher Gow

Ruzzetti & Gow, a company located in Manhattan, gathers shells from around the world, has them silver-coated in Rome, and turns them into dazzling candleholders, serving dishes, and other decorative pieces. The company hires artists to embellish furniture with shells; it also sells imported Asian furniture inlayed with delicate mother-of-pearl and Mediterranean red coral in all sizes. Christopher Gow, the company's founder, fashioned his New York apartment with so many shells that it feels more like a vacation retreat than most beach houses.

High style
The showroom, shown at far left on the facing page, features a variety of silver-coated shells. A shell mirror, an obelisk, a topiary, and red coral from the Mediterranean, shown at right on the facing page, are just a few of the stylish items offered by the company.

Diverse collection
Large silver-coated shells, shown at left, are used as sculptures or elegant serving dishes. A shell-decorated console table, mother-of-pearl boxes, and an oil painting, all shown above, display the company's diversity of shell-related items.

PROFILE
Christopher Gow's Collection

In 1995, Christopher Gow, then a specialist for Sotheby's, discovered an unusual collection of shell-encrusted furniture in an antique shop while traveling in the walled city of Carcassonne, France. He excitedly purchased the dazzling collection for what seemed to be a considerable sum, but eight months later, the amount was more than tripled at auction. Thus began a new passion and a new specialized business of sophisticated shell-related decorative home furnishings.

Louis XV style
A richly adorned console table, shown at top left, a dramatic female bust, shown at top right, and a shell-laden chest of drawers, pictured at bottom right, were all made in France during the early 18th century.

Precision harmony
An elaborate drop-front desk, shown on the facing page, has been painstakingly decorated in exquisite patterns. The piece was made in France, probably in the 1920s.

shells at the
TABLE

We admire shells for their intrinsic beauty, sometimes never even realizing that a soft-bodied animal known as a mollusk once lived inside. Mollusks have been a vital food source for thousands of years, since long before anyone collected them for tools or pleasure, and they continue to be a delicacy for many palates.

This chapter celebrates the gift of life that shellfish bring us and the rich pleasures and traditions of dishes and table decor made with these offerings from the sea.

Some of the wonderful shell-inspired fashions worn by guests
at the banquet include sun-loving sandals designed by Sophia
Slote, shown above; a whimsical bustier, shown at top right,
designed by Deborah McDowell and perfect for any mermaid's
wardrobe; and a stylish headdress, shown at bottom right,
designed by Susie Freeman. On the facing page, Chloë and
Phoebe Rohn wear shell-decorated dresses of their own design.

The table decor and recipes (see pages 147–49) described and shown in this chapter come from a scrumptious shell-motif banquet that I hosted for the contributors to this book. There is nothing like good eating to promote the unity of humankind, and the banquet was a celebration of my guests' artistry, the culinary delights of shellfish, and, of course, the fabulous shell in all its glory!

The banquet was held in an old barn. Fishing nets hung like drapery over a beam at the top of the stairs. Three long tables were covered in white linen and draped with off-white gauze. The centerpiece was an enormous clamshell filled with pink lilies, dillweed, and goatsbeard. In keeping with the soft color scheme, the chair backs were wrapped with delicate salmon pink fabric. Each place was set with a shell "plate" and a shell "glass."

Candleholders took their stately places on the banquet tables. Hovering above was an octopus chandelier, delightfully dangling its tentacles of candles. Mirrors covered in shells, a sailor's valentine, a shadow box of shell flowers, and incredible shell paintings by Ann Getsinger adorned the walls. Lamps with shell-veneered shades provided ambient lighting. All this and much more was created by the artists attending the banquet.

The mood was light and happy as the shell worshipers arrived in shell-bedecked attire, bearing platters of smoked mussels, steamed lobsters, oysters, clams, and crab cakes. Shells adorned their hats and shoes, dangled from their necks, and swung from their ears. The weather was humid but sunny, yet "rain" dripped from the corrugated metal roof of the barn (actually a practical cooling system designed by David Rothstein, the owner and architect of this grand structure). As the guests entered the barn, they rushed through the trickling water and ducked under the fishing nets, which added to the charming sea life atmosphere.

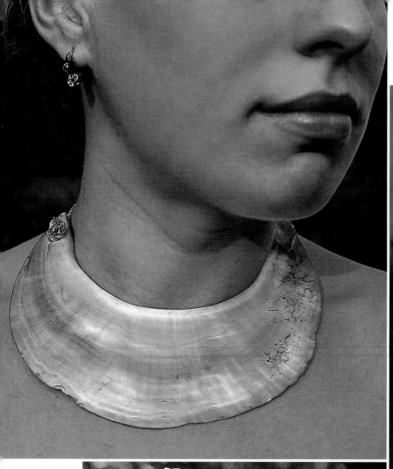

A kina shell, probably from Papua New Guinea, makes a spectacular necklace, shown at top left. A tropical shirt complements the shell hat worn by Reginald Madison, being greeted by me in the photo above. Shell-speckled shoes, shown at top right and designed by Janet Cooper, beg the question, "Shell we dance?" Helen Thomas and Egor Lasic, shown at right, toast their engagement with champagne-filled nautilus shells.

OYSTERS, ANYONE?

I grew up in an Irish Catholic family in Boston, and we had to eat fish every Friday as part of our religious duties. The menu varied each week and included fish-and-chips, steamers, mussels, and lobster. I loved it all and remember fondly those fish-filled Fridays! But, I must confess, there is one dish I could not bring myself to eat — raw oysters. For some reason, they looked awful, and I could only imagine that they tasted about the same as they looked. Then, while researching this book, I was invited to dinner by a friend. When I arrived, she proudly announced that we were having raw oysters as the appetizer. I admit that I panicked a little, but being an adult and involved in writing this book, I agreed to be brave and face my fear. And so I squeezed on some lemon juice, picked up the shell, and quickly slid the oyster into my mouth. To my surprise, its delicate, fresh flavor tingled in my mouth, and I was a convert.

The gathering was a spiritually uplifting experience, with people of all ages in attendance. There was a pleasant exchange of creative energies as we came together to acknowledge the fabulous, incomparable shell. I felt honored to have orchestrated this event and to have the pleasure of knowing such a wealth of creative artists.

Although our table settings were unique, using shells in tableware is nothing new. The Vikings cherished the giant green snail shell, which grew as large as 8 inches across. They removed the shell's rough outer layer and polished the inner surface to a smooth, iridescent, pearly finish. Next, they trimmed the shell with gold or silver, set jewels in the base, and used it as an elaborate royal drinking goblet or platter (some of these pieces can be seen at the Metropolitan Museum of Art in New York City).

In 1518, the Portuguese introduced porcelain to Europe. The French, who called cowrie shells *porcelaines,* used the same word to describe the fine wares made at such companies as Limoges and Minton. The composition of porcelain was a long-kept secret; people later discovered that it was made from marine shells and eggshells.

Versace designed a collection of tableware for Rosenthal called La Mer. The design is a royal blue rim that encircles a cluster of shells and red coral. Naturally, it would be the perfect tableware for seafood dishes.

MENU

Fried Oysters in Sesame Batter
Steamed Mussels in White Wine & Garlic
Clams Casino

Crab Cakes on a Bed of Arugula

Sautéed Bay Scallops with Ginger Cream Sauce over Penne
Butter-Poached Lobster with Fennel, Pancetta
& Pesto Vinaigrette
Sautéed Soft-Shell Crabs
Seafood Paella

Cheesecake with Belgian Chocolate Sea Life

PROFILE
Pamela Hardcastle

A floral and landscape designer, Pamela Hardcastle lives and works in western Massachusetts. She has been enriched by a variety of interests, including singing in a rhythm and blues band. Her need for outfits that allow free movement onstage led to a career in fashion design.

When Pamela had young children, she directed her creative efforts toward gardening, and then with the encouragement of a dear friend, she shifted her career to designing with flowers. She then created lovely floral arrangements for a local inn, as well as lavish ones for elaborate weddings. Focusing on her theme of "form and outline design," she now works these concepts into her exquisite table settings (left, below, and facing page) and outdoor arrangements (see pages 80 and 83). In Pamela's creative hands, the dance of shells in the landscape and shells matched with flowers are dreamy concoctions.

Shown above, rose petals, green beach glass, lion's paw shells, and a big starfish surround a large clamshell bearing lavender hyacinths. A garden table tray, shown at right, displays peach and yellow roses, large polished turban and nautilus shells, and sea fans on a bed of pink rose cup shells. The stunning table arrangement on the facing page has the feel of a still life oil painting. The tiered pewter centerpiece is topped with a silver candelabrum, then styled with pincushion flowers (which look like sea anemones), sea-green glass balls, roses, and shells.

ELEGANT
CHEESECAKES

Susan Morgan, owner and pastry chef of Elegant Cheesecakes in Half

Moon Bay, California, designs and bakes cakes for all occasions. For

her coastal-theme cakes, she re-creates the shapes and colors of shells

and sea life. She hand-sculpts and hand-paints each shell confection with

Belgian chocolate and

surrounds the cake

with edible sand, a

combination of fine

sugar and food color-

ing. She will even

match the sand to the

color theme of the

occasion. The end

result is a sumptuous,

totally edible fantasy.

candleholder Designed by Fritz Rohn

A painter, gardener extraordinaire, and dealer in fine antiques, Fritz Rohn has an eye for beauty and distinction that is beyond reproach. He studied art history before moving on to explore painting at the Art Students League of New York. For the past 20 years, he has been a collector and dealer in European paintings and furniture. He and his wife, Dana, own and operate Jennings and Rohn Antiques in Woodbury, Connecticut. This candleholder was inspired by a store display stand that Fritz found at a flea market.

Materials

Metal 12"-high display stand or old candelabra stand

Flexible screening

Heavy-gauge framing wire

Hot glue gun and glue sticks

Variety of shells

Mat knife or other sharp tool

Varnish or shellac (optional)

Paintbrush (optional)

Step 1. Attaching screening with wire "thread"

1. Using the display stand or old candelabra stand as armature, wrap it with screening and use wire as thread to weave back and forth through the mesh and pull it as close and as taut as possible to the armature. The mesh surface should conform as closely as possible to the shape of the armature, though the surface will be more rounded.

2. The mesh surface offers a fine base to hold hot glue. With the hot glue gun, apply glue to the shells and affix them to the armature, starting at the base and applying the largest ones first. The glue will readily flow through the wire mesh, firmly attaching the shells to the base once the glue dries. (Hold the shells in place for a few seconds until the glue solidifies enough to secure them.) Continue working up the stands until the entire mesh surface is covered.

3. At the top of the candleholder, glue large shells facing upward to hold a votive or pillar candle. Take care that very little of the glue is left exposed. Remove any visible glue with a mat knife.

4. If you would like the candleholder to have a glossy finish, apply varnish over the shells with a paintbrush.

Step 2. Attaching shells with hot glue

Robert Currey, the owner of Currey & Company in Atlanta, Georgia, has a love of natural materials. He brought that sensibility to the development of a line of shell-encrusted lighting fixtures, and this grotto chandelier is a spectacular example.

octopus chandelier Designed by Dana Jennings Rohn

This funky, one-of-a-kind creature looks like it just emerged from the sea — barnacles and all! The designer, Dana Jennings Rohn, is an artist for all time. She is a whiz at sewing, painting, building, cooking, and baking and is a whorl of creative energy. She credits her parents and grandparents with constantly reinforcing artistry and craftsmanship. In her spare time, she deals in fine antiques at the shop she shares with her husband.

shelling
OUT

Enjoying an outdoor living space – be it a garden, a backyard, or a deck – is one of the pleasures of fine weather, and adorning that space with organic elements increases its appeal. At their essence, shells help us maintain our connection to nature. Many cultures have had this same insight. The ancient Greeks decorated their gardens with shell groupings and lined ornamental fishponds with shells. In Venice, the Grand Canal boasts numerous palace gardens with shell motifs, and the city is home to Giovanni Bernini's famous *Triton Fountain*, which has a shell as the central feature.

> "I scavenged from those thrown-out shells from restaurants, because they are beautiful and because I have never seen the ocean."
>
> — Bodan Litnanski, Russian-born gardener and artist in his 70s who transforms trash into treasure

Shells are truly wonderful to include in your garden, but I need to warn you of one hazard. It seems that raccoons like the smell of food that some shells retain. Some time ago, I covered a very large urn with cockleshells collected on Sanibel Island and planted it with a full array of herbs. Each morning thereafter, I woke up to find several shells pulled off the urn and trailed down the stairway on my deck. I reglued the shells and wondered what on earth was going

As shown on the facing page, a regal birdbath made by William Schade towers over its flowery domain. He also created the cement leaves that twist around the column. The garden design by Pamela Hardcastle, shown above, features a rustic urn filled with succulents surrounding a large, half-opened clamshell, while large conch shells dance around the base. At right, a gazing ball, resting atop an elegant base made by William Schade, stands tall to meet the approaching eyes of all who enter this enchanted garden.

on, because the exterior silicone adhesive that I had used was very strong and able to withstand all types of weather.

At first, I thought one of my three cats was using the urn as a clawing area, but then one evening around dusk, I looked out and saw a very brave raccoon heading toward my precious shells. I chased him away, and after a few evenings of seeing me fume toward him, he seemed to lose interest. This was a good choice on the raccoon's part, because I was willing to fight the fight to protect my work!

A Victorian miniature shell castle, shown at left, is small in size but not in stature. I salvaged the three-tiered plant stand, shown above, from the dump; it sparkles with new life now that scallop shells have been glued to the rims. Robin Greeson designed the garden table, shown at right, from a thick sheet of copper. Four large conch shells dangle from strong wire secured through holes drilled in the table, while my cat, Pearl, surveys the scene.

birdbath
Designed by Marlene Hurley Marshall

For this birdbath, I used a large display bowl purchased from a department store and a larger-than-usual drainpipe made of clay and painted dark brown. Because the bowl was so large, I needed a solid, ample base to support it. The unadorned birdbath sat in my yard for many years; now, with a basketful of shells and some glue, it has been transformed into a fanciful garden ornament that is beautiful as well as practical.

Materials

Birdbath and pedestal

Several containers of silicone caulk

Ratchet gun

12 lion's paw shells

Large number and variety of shells

Iridescent abalone slices

Green mercury glass ball

Green and white beach glass

1. Set the birdbath bowl on the pedestal and work on the inside surface first. Use silicone caulk in a ratchet gun to attach shells approximately 5 inches apart. To achieve the design shown, first attach large lion's paw shells. Then place two large bivalves below each one to provide support, almost like feet.

Step 1. Gluing shells to the inside of the birdbath bowl

Fill the spaces in between with a variety of medium-sized shells to create a 5-inch border. Let the glue dry for 24 hours.

Step 2. Gluing shells to the bottom of the bowl

2. Turn the bowl over. Do not glue any shells to the center of the bowl bottom or to the lip, so that the bowl will rest flat and firmly on the base. Spread silicone caulk over the rest of the surface and cover the outer rim with slices of iridescent abalone shells. Cover the entire underside with medium and small shells, then let the silicone dry for 24 hours.

3. Turn the bowl right side up, resting the bottom on the pedestal. To achieve the design shown, glue a green mercury glass ball in the center of the bowl, then surround it with green and white beach glass.

4. To decorate the pedestal, trim the lower rim with turban shells (the ones featured here, purchased from a dealer, were sanded in a swirl pattern to reveal the undercoat of mother-of-pearl). Gluing on these shells is fairly easy, because the small lip on the base of the pedestal supports them. Using this first line of shells for support, build the design upward. Large cockleshells (bought at the Sanibel shell sale!) and borders of green beach glass help tie the design on the pedestal to that on the bowl.

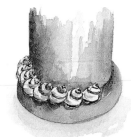

Step 4. Gluing shells to the lower rim of the pedetsal

Birdhouse

The birdhouse at left was designed by Ron Ronan, who is an artist, designer, and decorative painter. He built it from birch wood and bark and covered it with shells collected on family vacations, along with antique tintypes, metal typesetting characters, and a tag sale ceramic bird.

Ron's fine artwork is mostly collage, with writing, old photographs, letters, and numbers attached to a base of encaustic (wax that is melted and applied to the surface) mixed with acrylic pigments. Ron is part of the design team for his wife's business, Elements/Jill Schwartz, which produces picture frames, journals, photo albums, and address books.

Shell-Covered Vertebrae

John Slauson's shell-covered vertebrae, shown at right, make a unique sculptural element. John's craftsmanship is well used in his work as a properties artist for theater productions, which requires woodworking, sculpting, crafting, welding, and just about everything else. His main emphasis is on mixed-media metal sculpture. John made this piece, *Endoskeleton/Exoskeleton,* with a single goal in mind — to create a skeleton that, in some odd way, looked as though it could exist in nature. He says, "I wanted the shellwork to be indistinct, so that it would not be obvious what had been done to the bones. My wish is that an archaeologist will find this piece in the ground a thousand years from now — and be baffled."

blooms of the sea
Designed by Goz Gosselin

When discussing garden elements, we cannot forget the fabulous flower; and when flowers are made from shells in the hands of a talented artist, the results can be extraordinary! Allow me to introduce you to shell flower master Goz Gosselin. A retired florist from Connecticut who spends a great deal of time designing fabulous and fanciful flower arrangements, Goz is a designer and artist of the highest level.

Goz's basically self-taught, painstaking craftsmanship is reflected in his penchant for miniature forms, even though he designs in all sizes. Goz and his wife, Terri, assemble their creations for admiring clients while ensconced at their winter home in Fort Myers, Florida, before returning to their home in Connecticut each summer. Goz has won numerous first-place awards for his designs, and he shares his vast and wonderful store of knowledge in the instructions for this simple shell flower arrangement. This is a multiple-step process that includes assembling the platform stems, making shell dust and chips, making the shell flowers, and arranging the shell flowers.

assembling platform stems

Materials

Wire cutters

30-gauge green cotton-covered wire

Round needle-nosed pliers

Note: The shells used in this project are all bivalves and have a right and a left side. Sort the shells by size and by sides. If these shells are not available, others of the same size can be used.

1. Using wire cutters, cut the 30-gauge wire into 187 lengths of 5 inches each.

2. Place one piece of wire on the tip of the pliers and turn it once around them to form a loop.

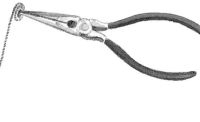

Step 3. Creating a spiral for the platform stem

3. Put the wire loop into the pinch of the pliers and rotate the wire to continue the spiral, creating the platform stem. The completed platform resembles the end of a fiddle head fern (see illustration). The size of the platform depends on the size of the shells used. Usually, two or three spirals will suffice for the flowers in this project.

4. After the platform is shaped, bring the wire back to the center, lay it flat against the platform, and bend it so it is perpendicular to the wire stem.

5. Repeat steps 2 through 4 with each of the remaining 186 lengths of wire and set them aside.

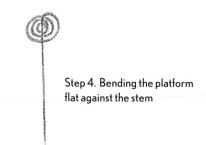

Step 4. Bending the platform flat against the stem

Shell Flower Centerpiece

Goz Gosselin designed this show-stopper, which won two top awards, including "Best Flower Exhibit," at the Sanibel Shell Fair. It is one of his larger pieces and took 150 hours to complete. The purple-blue tulips are made from three large clamshells, and their center "stamens" are made from three tusk shells tipped with yellow shell dust. The white flowers, similar to Gloriosa lilies, are made from the hinges of duck clams, and the peach-colored sprays are made from periwinkle shells and look like bleeding heart. Slices of conch shells wired to long stems provide visual interest, and sprays of artificial golden rod coated with yellow shell dust complete the arrangement.

making shell dust and chips

Materials

Dust mask

Eye protection

Duck clams or other fragile white shells

Measuring cup

Old blender (pick one up from a garage sale)

3 sieves with different sizes of mesh (a tea strainer is good as the smallest)

3 containers

Several self-sealing sandwich-sized plastic bags

Tablespoon

Green, yellow, and white acrylic paints

Paper

Note: Never return the colored dust or chips to the blender, as this breaks them down again and you will end up with a speckled effect rather than a solid color. Since you now have a supply of small and large chips, you may use either one in the center of each flower. The small chips work better on the smaller flowers.

Note: Since shell dust is harmful to the lungs, always wear a mask when working with it. Eye protection is also a good idea when you are using a blender.

1. With your hands, break the duck clams into small pieces. Remove the hard hinge area and save it for another use. Place ¼ cup of the broken shells in the blender, cover it, and blend for 10 seconds.

2. Place the broken shells in a sieve with the smallest mesh holes, and shake it over a container to catch the tiniest shell chips, which I call shell dust.

Step 2. Sifting shell dust

3. Repeat the process with the medium-mesh sieve, collecting the small shell chips in a separate container. Repeat again with the large sieve, collecting the large shell chips in a separate container.

4. Put the shell pieces that do not fall through the last sieve back into the blender, add another ¼ cup of broken duck clams, and begin the process again. You now have a supply of shell dust, small chips, and large chips.

Step 5. Coloring shell dust

5. Place ½ cup of dust in a plastic bag. Add 1 tablespoon of green acrylic paint (or yellow acrylic paint for the Shellwork Shadow Box project that follows). Seal the bag. Do not put a lot of paint into the bag, because it will make the dust or chips turn into a big glob. In this case, less is more. Knead the bag to thoroughly color the dust, then spread the colored shell mixture on a sheet of clean paper to dry. When thoroughly dry, sift it in the smallest sieve and discard the pieces that don't pass through.

6. Repeat this process to color the small chips yellow and the large chips white.

making shell flowers

Materials

High-temperature glue pot

Hot glue (type recommended by the glue pot's manufacturer)

22 small pink apple-blossom shells

Tweezers

187 platform stems
(see directions on page 90)

Shallow container

Small artist's brush (#10/0)

White glue

Green shell dust
(see directions on page 93)

Teaspoon

Yellow shell chips
(see directions on page 93)

171 small to medium pink
apple-blossom shells

159 small to medium purple
cay cay shells

White shell chips
(see directions on page 93)

66 small to medium white
coquina shells

Vase (this could actually be a shell)

Bond 527

Small stones

Styrofoam

Florist adhesive

Dried moss

16- and 20-gauge green
cotton-covered wire

¼" florist tape, cut in half
lengthwise

Silk foliage

1. Turn on the glue pot and heat a scant amount of glue. Do not over-fill the pot, as you want only a little glue on each shell.

2. To make the apple-blossom buds, separate the 22 small pink apple-blossom shells into 11 pairs of matching sizes. Pick up one shell with tweezers and lightly dip the hinged end into the hot glue. Using your fingers to guide its placement, lay the shell on the outer ring of a platform stem, then place a second shell next to it. Repeat to make 11 buds.

Step 2. Attaching two shells
to a platform stem to make
an apple-blossom bud

3. Hold a shallow container under the bud. Dip the artist's brush in white glue and paint the underside of the bud, the platform, and a slight amount of the shell's edge to strengthen the bud. While the glue is still wet, sprinkle on green shell dust with a teaspoon to form the miniature calyx of the bud. Collect the dust that has fallen into the

container and use it for the next bud. Let the flowers dry for 2 hours before going on to the next step.

Step 3. Coating bud base
with green shell dust

4. With the artist's brush, place a small amount of white glue in the center of each bud; sprinkle yellow shell chips onto the wet glue. Collect the extra chips for later use. Set the buds aside until the glue is dry (about 2 hours).

5. To make the medium apple-blosson flowers, separate the 171 pink apple-blossom shells into 57 groups of three matching shells. Repeat steps 2, 3, and 4 to create these flowers, using three shells instead of two for each flower. Overlap each shell a bit as you glue it to the platform stem. Let these flowers dry for 2 hours.

6. To make the cay cay shell flowers, separate the 159 purple cay cay shells into 53 groups of three matching shells. Repeat the same steps as for the medium apple-blossom flowers, using three shells per flower and overlapping them slightly. Use large white shell chips for the center of each flower. Let these flowers dry for 2 hours.

Step 6. Making three-petaled cay cay flowers

7. To make the coquina flowers, glue each of the 66 white coquina shells onto its own platform stem. Dip the artist's brush into the white glue and paint the underside of each flower, the platform, and a slight amount of the shell's edge. While the glue is still wet, sprinkle on green dust with a teaspoon, using a shallow container to catch the excess. Let the flowers dry for 2 hours.

8. To prepare the vase, use Bond 527 to glue small stones to the inside bottom of the container. Since shell flowers tend to be top-heavy, the stones add weight to the bottom. Let the container dry overnight.

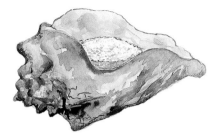

Step 9. Styrofoam being secured inside shallow shell vase

9. Cut a piece of Styrofoam to fit snugly inside the vase. Secure the Styrofoam to the inside of the vase with florist adhesive. Cover the top of the Styrofoam with moss.

10. To assemble the flowers, make a small hydrangea by combining three of the apple-blossom buds and 11 of the apple-blossom flowers. Use a 1-foot length of 16-gauge wire and florist tape to hold the buds and flowers together. Add small pieces of silk foliage to the bottom of each flower.

Step 10. Making a small hydrangea

11. Following the instructions in step 10, assemble a medium-sized hydrangea using four apple-blossom buds and 18 apple-blossom flowers.

12. Following the instructions in step 10, assemble a large hydrangea with four apple-blossom buds and 28 apple-blossom flowers.

13. Separate the 53 cay cay flowers into five groups of 5, 8, 9, 13, and 18. Bend each flower at the calyx as if it were bowing its head, much like a lily-of-the-valley. Using a 1-foot length of 20-gauge cotton-covered wire and florist tape, assemble the five cay cay sprays, placing smaller flowers at the top and graduating them. Each will be a different size.

Step 13. Assembling one spray of cay cay flowers

14. Separate the 66 coquina flowers into seven groups of 3, 4, 8, 9, 10, 11, and 21. Using a 1-foot length of 20-gauge cotton-covered wire and florist tape, assemble each of the seven coquina sprays, placing smaller flowers at the top and graduating them in size.

Step 14. Assembling one spray of coquina flowers

arranging
shell flowers

Materials

Shell flowers
(see directions on pages 94–95)

Ruler or measuring tape

Wire cutters

Wired wooden 4" floral picks

Florist tape

White glue

Silk foliage

1. Take the smallest of the three hydrangeas and measure and cut the wire stem to a 10-inch length. Place a 4-inch wooden pick on the end, wrap the wire with florist tape, and dip it in white glue. Stick the wire end through the moss and Styrofoam and position the hydrangea in the center of the container.

2. Repeat the process with the medium-sized hydrangea, positioning it below the small hydrangea.

3. Repeat the process with the large hydrangea, positioning it below the medium-sized one.

4. Repeat the process with the tallest cay cay spray, positioning it to one side of the hydrangea grouping, then repeat the process with the four other sprays.

5. Looking at the photo of the project, arrange the remaining flowers accordingly. Remember to dip each stem in white glue before inserting it into the Styrofoam.

6. Add the silk foliage as an accent. Don't overdo it with the artificial greenery, as the shell flowers should be the predominant feature of the arrangement.

As shown at left, a magnificent bouquet of shell flowers designed by Goz Gosselin has a realistic appearance that reflects his background as a florist before he retired and danced with shells. Goz often designs exotic fantasy creations, such as the amazing topiary shown at right.

shellwork shadow box
Designed by Goz Gosselin

Making a shellwork shadow box gives you a great deal of creative freedom, as its three dimensions provide plenty of space to explore. Try using odd shells, sea glass, sea plants, driftwood, coral, and smooth stones to create anything from a collage beach scene to a delicate flower arrangement. This is a multiple-step process that includes making the shadow box frame, assembling the platform stems, making shell dust and chips, making the shell flowers, and arranging the shell flowers.

making the shadow box frame

Materials

Pane of glass cut a tad smaller than the frame

Rubbing alcohol

Ruler or measuring tape

Premade wooden shadow box (7" x 14" x 1¾")

Professional mat cutter or straightedge and T square

30" x 30" piece of ³⁄₁₆"-thick foam core

30" x 30" piece of mat board (preferably acid free)

White glue

Weights (heavy books work well)

Flat shell for base

2"-thick sheet of Styrofoam

Utility knife

Tacky glue

Note: The size of the shadow box is your personal choice. You can purchase a ready-made shadow box frame at a craft store or make an existing frame deeper by adding wood to the sides. These instructions use a shadow box that is 1¾ inches deep, 7 inches wide, and 14 inches tall.

1. Clean the glass with rubbing alcohol and place it in the frame.

2. Measure the length of the inside edges of the frame. Using a professional mat cutter or a straightedge and T square, measure and cut four 1½-inch-wide strips of foam core and of mat board to fit snugly inside the frame.

Step 3. Sliding glue-coated foam core into box

3. Place the foam core in the frame; this is what holds the glass down. (Make sure you have a snug fit, so the glass doesn't move.) Place the top and bottom, then the

sides; check the fit. Remove all four pieces of foam core and apply white glue to them, keeping the glue away from the edges. Insert the pieces into the frame and press down firmly.

4. Place the cut mat board strips on top of the foam core strips and check the fit. (Follow the same procedure you used for the foam core: Fit the top and bottom first, then the sides.) Remove all four pieces of mat board and glue them to the foam core with white glue. Make sure that the corners butt up against each other for a neat and perfect fit with no gaps. You should now have a ¼-inch-deep ridge all around the inside edge of the frame; this is where the back mat will sit.

5. To obtain the measurements for the back mat, measure the inside edge of the frame and subtract ⅛ inch from the length and the height. Cut a piece each of foam core and mat board to that size. This will be the back of the box. Glue the foam core and mat board together, applying white glue to the outside edges first and then in squiggles down the middle. Place weights on top so it doesn't curl up, and let it dry for 2 or more hours.

6. To prepare the shell base for your flower arrangement, select a shell that isn't too deep to fit in the frame but has enough space for a small piece of Styrofoam to fit inside it. Use a utility knife to cut an appropriate-sized piece of Styrofoam.

7. Measure and mark the center of the back mat, then use tacky glue to affix the Styrofoam to it. Glue the shell on top of the Styrofoam. Let everything dry overnight.

Step 7. Attaching shell base to Styrofoam

making shell flowers

Materials

45 medium off-white coquina shells and 36 small peach coquina shells to make nine coquina flowers

High-temperature glue pot

Hot glue recommended by glue pot manufacturer

Tweezers

35 platform stems (see page 90)

Artist's brush (#10/0)

White glue

Green shell dust (see page 93)

Teaspoon

Shallow container

Small yellow shell chips (see page 93)

18 medium zebra mussels and 18 small zebra mussels to make six irises

Yellow shell dust (see page 93)

78 small garfish scales to make 13 gar flowers

White shell chips

21 medium cup shells to make seven cup flowers

Mustard seeds

Note: If these shells and/or fish scales are not available, use something similar.

1. To make the coquina flowers, separate the 45 medium off-white coquinas into nine groups of five and the 36 small peach coquinas into nine groups of four (match the size of shells for each group).

2. Turn on the glue pot and heat a scant amount of glue. Do not over-fill the pot, as you want only a small amount of glue on each shell.

3. Use tweezers to pick up an off-white coquina and dip the hinged end into the hot glue, placing a scant amount of glue on the shell. Place the shell on the outer ring of a platform stem, then glue a second shell next to it in a circular fashion. Repeat until all five off-white shells are in place. Overlap each shell a little as you place it on the platform. Put aside each one as you finish it.

Step 4. Making coquina flowers from five medium off-white shells and four small peach shells

4. After you have completed the outer ring of off-white petals, attach an inner ring of small peach

coquinas, overlapping them in the same manner as the first row, but using only four shells this time. Finish all nine coquina flowers.

5. Dip the artist's brush in white glue and paint the underside of the flower, the platform, and a slight amount of the shell edges to help strengthen the flower. While the glue is still wet, sprinkle on green shell dust with a teaspoon. Do this over a shallow container to collect the dust and use it for the next flower. Let the flowers dry for 2 hours.

6. Place a small amount of white glue in the center of the flower and sprinkle it with yellow shell chips.

7. To make the irises, separate the 18 medium zebra mussels into six groups of three and the 18 small zebra mussels into six groups of three (match shell sizes for each group).

8. Use tweezers to dip the hinged part of the medium zebra mussel into the glue pot, placing a scant amount of glue on it. Place the shell on the edge of the platform stem with the hollow opening facing inward and hanging below the platform, then repeat with the two other medium zebra mussels. Space the shells evenly around the platform edge. Put aside each one as you finish it.

9. After you have completed the bottom ring petals, glue the three small zebra mussels on top of the platform in an upward fashion with the hollow opening facing inward, spacing them between the lower shells. Finish all nine flowers, then repeat step 5 to sprinkle green shell dust on them.

Step 9. Iris flower from six zebra mussels

10. Using the artist's brush, paint white glue in small strips tapering to a point on the lower petals. Sprinkle the area with yellow shell dust to create the beard of the iris.

Step 11. Gar flowers from six garfish scales

11. To make the gar flowers, separate the 78 gar scales into 13 groups of six. Pick up the scale with tweezers, dip the pointed end into the glue pot, and place the scale in a circular fashion on top of the platform stem. Repeat with the five remaining scales. Finish all 13 flowers, then repeat step 5 to sprinkle green shell dust on them. Let the flowers dry for 2 hours.

12. Place a small dab of white glue in the center of the flower and sprinkle it with white shell chips.

13. To make the cup flowers, separate the 21 cup shells into seven groups of three. Glue the hinge onto the platform stem, overlapping the shell with the next one. Finish all seven flowers, then repeat step 5 to sprinkle green shell dust in the center of each one.

Step 14. Making cup flower from three cup shells, green shell dust, and mustard seeds

14. Place a small dab of white glue in the center of the flower and sprinkle it with mustard seeds.

AN EXTRAORDINARY TRIBUTE

In 1948, George Howard of Dorset, England, began creating an extraordinary shell garden in memory of his son Michael, who had died of meningitis at the age of 14. George added to the garden every year for nearly 50 years, constructing pieces that looked very much like flower beds joined by mosaic paths, as well as a tiled grotto and shrines with Jesus and Buddha statues.

The shell-encrusted walls contained rocks from Iceland, coral from South Africa, and thousands of shells collected by George during his travels as a merchant seaman. Purported to be worth more than half a million dollars, the shell garden was enjoyed by tourists during the many years that George worked on it.

The garden was featured in many international publications as an important visionary environment. However, because it was not listed as a historic site, the garden was not protected by the state. After George died, his other son, Raymond, ordered that the shell garden be demolished in a secret operation, leaving many people outraged that a much-loved landmark had been destroyed.

arranging the flowers

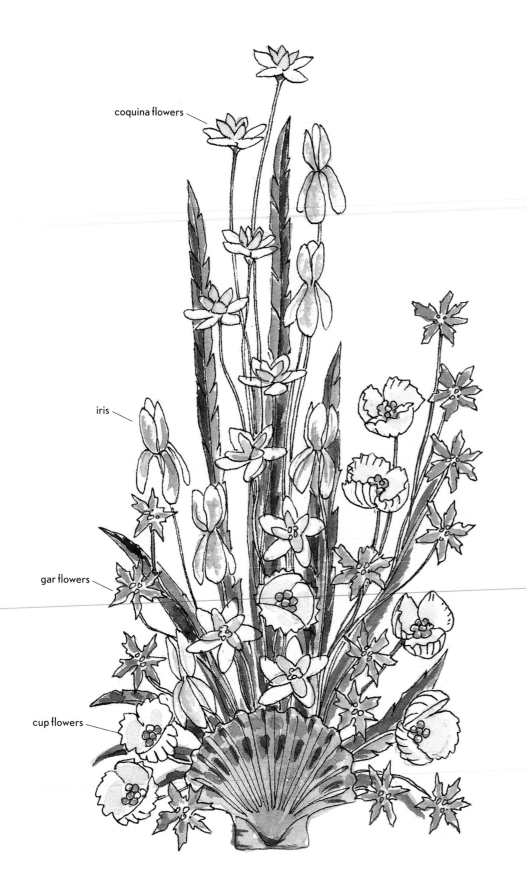

coquina flowers

iris

gar flowers

cup flowers

Materials

Florist adhesive

16-gauge green cotton-covered wire

Shell flowers (see pages 100–101)

White glue

Shadow box (see pages 98–99)

Miniature silk foliage

Framing stapler

Brown wrapping paper

Frame hangers and wires

Note: Be careful not to drip glue onto the mat board, and make sure your hands are clean prior to starting this portion of the project. You can use the illustration and instructions here and arrange the flowers accordingly or experiment with your own design.

1. Using the florist adhesive and a 6-inch piece of 16-gauge wire, assemble seven of the coquina flowers in a scattered row to create a spray of flowers, placing smaller ones at the top and graduating them in size. Dip the ends of the wire in white glue and insert them into the Styrofoam behind the shell attached to the back mat of the shadow box. These will be the tallest flowers in the center of the arrangement. Place the two remaining coquina flowers singly into the Styrofoam behind the shell.

2. Make two sprays of three irises each and repeat the procedure, placing them in the arrangement (see illustration at left).

3. Make one spray of seven gar flowers and one of three gar flowers (this leaves three single gar flowers). The spray of seven flowers goes to the far right of the arrangement, the spray of three flowers goes to the far left, and the remaining single flowers are placed where needed to fill space.

4. Make a spray of three cup flowers (this leaves four single cup flowers). Place the spray to the right, between the main coquina spray and the gar flower spray. The remaining four cup flowers are placed where needed or as seen in the illustration on the facing page.

5. Remove any small particles of shell chips that may have fallen. Add some silk foliage as an accent to the shell flowers, and set the box aside to dry overnight.

6. Sign your name in the lower corner of the mat and place the back mat with the shell arrangement into the shadow box. Attach it to the frame with the framing stapler.

7. Seal the back with brown wrapping paper and attach frame hangers and wire.

Pages 104–105: Another shadow box creation by Goz Gosselin displays a scallop-shell picket fence enclosing a shell flower garden of roses; irises; lilies of the valley; and spiky, daisylike, and star-shaped flowers. The green foliage is made of quilling paper cut to resemble small ferns. This piece won the blue ribbon in the "Flower Picture" division of the Sanibel Shell Fair.

THE JERSEY
SHELL GARDEN

In 1957, Colin Soudain began constructing a dramatic shell garden, using local shells, mainly mother-of-pearl, collected from the shores of his native island of Jersey, one of the islands in the English Channel. The garden features shells embedded in dark red cement and has a religious theme, with many crosses and altars made of shells. As Colin's energy flagged, his nephew, John Morgan, gradually took over the project. He added his own spiritual messages from well-known leaders, including the line from a John Lennon song, "People say I'm a dreamer, but I'm not the only one."

Today, John feels that the garden is a special place for peace and meditation, because it expresses a unity between people and nature. He plans to build a waterfall and a shell bridge to create a rain forest atmosphere. The shell garden is open to the public for a small fee.

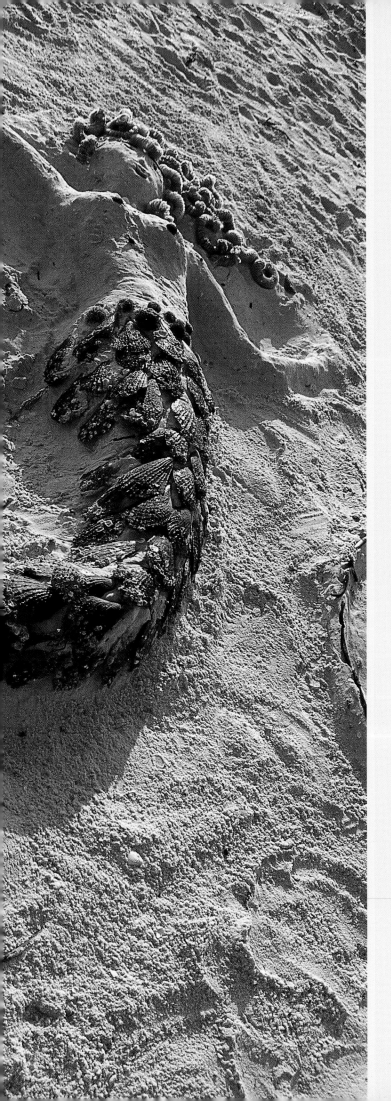

sharing
shells with
KIDS

When I introduced shells to my five-year-old grandson Quinn, he was immediately taken. Up to that point, his main interest had been dinosaurs. As we looked at a shell dictionary with wonderful large photographs of every shell imaginable, he likened shells to dinosaurs, and, of course, his instincts were correct.

Shells are a great subject to share with kids, and a visual guide to shells can be a lifetime educational tool. When kids are armed with a little information and a lot of curiosity, beach-combing can become a playful new game of "Name That Shell" and a treasure hunt for objects to use in child-oriented projects.

"It is fascinating to consider the contribution to the life of the world that the simple shell has made."

—Louise Travers

stegosaurus
wind chimes

Designed by Quinn James Doherty

My grandson Quinn, who adores dinosaurs and baseball, has become a shell collector and a recipient of many shell gifts. His grandfather Jim Scrimgeour wrote the poem "Sand Dollars" that appears on page 132. Quinn spends his summers on the coast of Maine and has already amassed a large shell collection.

stegosaurus wind chimes

Materials

Needle-nosed pliers

2 wire coat hangers or metal picture frame wire

Wire cutters

Nylon fishing line

½" or ¾" red and black ribbon

Glue gun and glue sticks

Small shells, preferably with holes in them

Small hand drill with fine carbide bit (if shells do not have holes)

Household needle with large eye

Scissors

4 red pipe cleaners

4 auger shells

Thin wire

Note: Younger children will need parental assistance, especially to work the glue gun and bend the coat hanger into shape.

1. With a pair of needle-nosed pliers, untwist two coat hangers. Shape one hanger into the dinosaur's body, then twist the ends together.

2. With wire cutters, cut the second coat hanger in half. Make five spikes in one of the pieces (this will be the dinosaur's back). Secure the spikes to the dinosaur with fishing line at each bend.

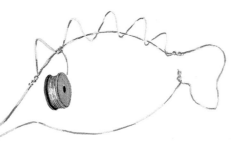

Step 2. Securing spikes with fishing line

3. Shape the other half into a circle and twist the ends together. Secure the circle between the center top and bottom of the dinosaur frame to create the stomach, with the circle at a 90-degree angle to create a three-dimensional effect. Secure the circle in place with fishing line.

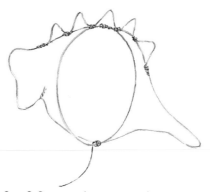

Step 3. Securing the center circle with fishing line

4. Working from the head to the tail, wrap the spikes with red ribbon, securing it with dabs of hot glue as you wrap.

5. Wrap the dinosaur's body and belly with black ribbon, securing the ribbon with dabs of hot glue as you wrap.

6. If the shells do not already have small holes in them, use a small drill with a fine carbide bit to drill holes at the top of each one.

7. Thread the needle with fishing line and sew through the ribbon at the top of the dinosaur frame. In the space between the top and the bottom of the frame, drop a long length of fishing line (make the length twice the size of the body to allow for adjustments in the knots for each shell). Cut the line with scissors and make a knot in the top. Repeat the process to make ten lines that graduate in length, with the shortest lines at the tail and the head and the longest line in the center of the body.

8. Slide a shell onto the center fishing line and tie a knot about ½ inch from the top of the shell. Repeat the process, sliding on shells and tying knots in the fishing line to leave a space of about ½ inch between shells. Complete the line, which should hold three or four shells, depending on their size and the length of the line. Repeat the

Steps 7 & 8. Sewing fishing line through ribbon and threading shells on line

process on the lines on each side of the center line, this time suspending two or three shells on the shorter lengths. At the tail and neck of the dinosaur, suspend one shell on each line. Drop another length of line in the center of the head and hang one shell for the eye. Cut off the excess fishing line.

9. Suspend two fishing lines inside the dinosaur's stomach (make sure they won't get tangled with the other lines) and repeat step 8 with these lines.

10. Bend each pipe cleaner into the shape of a foot and wrap all four around the bottom of the dinosaur's body, placing two feet at the base of the frame near the center and the other two on the bottom center of the circle.

11. With hot glue, attach four auger shells to the base of the tail. Attach a wire on top to hang the wind chimes.

The child in all of us has memories of time spent at the beach building sand castles and collecting shells. Family holidays at the seashore can become wonderful opportunities for learning and creating, because there is so much to discover about shells. Children also have an open, spontaneous interest in the natural world and can appreciate the intricate beauty of shells as well as the tiny creatures that live inside them.

Shell Dolls

A vintage shell doll (top right) holds a tiny shell flower bouquet. Janet Cooper made contemporaty versions (bottom left) from her vast collection of wonderful objects. The larger doll has a papier-mâché head, plastic shoes, and a vintage hand-knitted baby sweater. Scallop shells form the dress and hands. The smaller doll has a photo-transfer face and clothing made from vintage fabrics with shells sewn onto them. Janet also made the framed picture (bottom right) by sewing and gluing shells and old doll heads onto fabric. She glued the fabric picture to the center of a box and glued a vintage shell frame to the rim, creating a shadow box effect. For more of Janet's work, see page 28.

Driftwood Shelf

Janice Shields works with grapevines and twigs to create interesting trellises for the garden. For this project, she collected driftwood from a beach on Cape Cod and created a rustic shelf as a natural place to display shell collections and beach treasures. Janice screwed the twigs and bleached driftwood together, creating a gradation in sizes from small to large, and attached screw eyes and wire to the back so it could be hung on a wall.

Chloë's and Phoebe's inspiration for their dollhouse, shown at right, came from the smaller Victorian shell house, above, that belonged to their great-great-grandmother.

shell dollhouse
Designed by Chloë and Phoebe Rohn

Chloë and Phoebe, who were 8 and 7 when they made this dollhouse, attend a Montessori school, study piano and ballet, and are budding antique dealers. These two young artists are the daughters of Fritz and Dana Rohn (see pages 75 and 120). With the guidance and influence of their talented parents, Chloë and Phoebe are well on their way to a creative lifestyle. They made this dollhouse from scratch, but you could instead cover an existing dollhouse that is sturdy enough to hold shells.

Materials

Plywood

Saw

Wood glue and old paintbrush

Screw gun

Small wood screws

4 cabinet knobs

White paint and paintbrush

Mortar and pestle

Jingle shells

Black sand

Hot glue gun

Scallop shells, mini cat's paw shells, large spindle shells

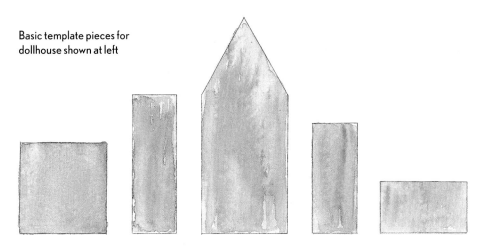

Basic template pieces for dollhouse shown at left

1. Decide the shape of the dollhouse and draw templates for the pieces. Cut the pieces out of plywood with a saw and assemble the structure with wood glue, a screw gun, and wood screws. Attach cabinet knobs with glue or screws to create feet and give the house more of a presence. Apply a coat of white paint inside and out.

2. Use a mortar and pestle to crush small jingle shells, which are very thin. Paint a thick coat of wood glue on the walls of the outside of the house. Lay the house on its side and press a thick layer of crushed shells onto the facing side. Allow each side to dry before turning the dollhouse and gluing shells onto another side. Apply crushed shells to all sides of the house.

3. Spread wood glue on the inside walls. Cover them with liberal amounts of black sand, then create a pattern with your fingers to resemble wallpaper.

4. Use a hot glue gun to apply scallop shells as roof shingles. Start at the bottom edge of the roof and move up, overlapping each layer. Glue a border of mini cat's paws along the front edges and the ridgeline. Glue large spindle shells as finials.

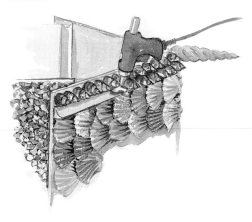

Step 4. Gluing mini cat's paws along front edge

dollhouse furniture   Designed by Chloë and Phoebe Rohn

Chloë and Phoebe used a variety of shells and a hot glue gun to design each piece of furniture for their dollhouse. Without any assistance, they worked out how to create a bed, a table, chairs, and even a tiny chandelier with wire and birthday candles. Chloë designed most of the dining room furniture, and Phoebe did the bedroom set. The sisters worked well together on their wonderful winter's evening project, dreaming of the sea as snow fell around their house.

A table, shown at top right, is made of a flat oyster shell held up by cone shells set atop cockle shells. Tiny jingle shells act as plates. Other furnishings, shown at top left, include a three-poster bed with a fan mussel canopy held aloft by auger shells and a cradle with an oyster shell mattress.

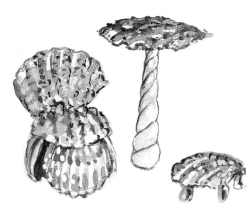

Chair, side table, and footstool

Materials

Selection of shells

Hot glue gun

For chandelier (pictured on page 106): wire, birthday candles, and screw eye (to hang chandelier, with assistance from an adult)

Dining table with plates

Canopy of three-poster bed

PROFILE
The Rohn Family

The Rohn family of Milton, Connecticut, is incredible in many ways. All four members collect shells and made projects for this book. Dana unabashedly fashioned the Octopus Chandelier (pages 78–79). She says hers is actually a "sexopus," with six arms. Fritz took on the challenge of making an extravagant candleholder (see page 75). From the workshop of Chloë and Phoebe burst forth a fantasy dollhouse, along with shell furniture and a chandelier.

In a preview of the latest shell apparel, Dana danced into the banquet in a dress featuring swirling waves of crushed shells, and Chloë and Phoebe wore their own shell-decorated dresses. To make their dresses, they spread Sobo fabric glue, which stays flexible, onto the fabric in the shape of the design, sprinkled pulverized jingle shells onto the glue, and pressed the pieces into the fabric. After it dried, they shook out the dresses to remove loose shells.

INNER CHAMBERS

Jules Verne's *Twenty Thousand Leagues under the Sea* was inspired by the chambered nautilus shell. The story is about a French scientist who loved shells and traveled in a fabulous underwater vehicle, called the Nautilus, that could dive into the depths of the sea and rise to the surface when needed. The book was written in 1870, some 30 years before the U.S. Navy acquired its first submarine.

The nautilus mollusk surely inspired Verne's fantasy of a seafaring vessel that could submerge and resurface at will. With amazing precision, this animal outgrows the first chamber it creates, then another chamber, then another — and each new chamber is exactly one-third larger than the previous one. In addition, it uses a siphon to fill the discarded chambers with 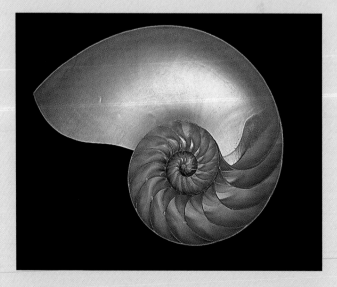 fluid when it wishes to submerge to the depths of its shell; when it wishes to rise to the surface, it empties the chambers, which then fill with air.

STARFISHER

Scott Clark is a dedicated musician, painter, and writer. He wrote "Starfisher" while living in a vintage cabin in the Berkshire hills of western Massachusetts. While writing, Scott was inspired to decorate his cabin window with shells, which further enhanced his creative process. The following is an excerpt from his story.

Jinjin, sulking in the bottom of his boat, hadn't caught a single fish; not a red, not a green, not a colour in between. He thought thoughts about his Mama, his eccentric father's quest, Old Turtle's odd capacities, and the one he loved the best — Leilani. In the meantime, he peered over the side of his boat and focused on the stars reflecting from the surface of the sea. Swirling a hand in the water as if to corral them, he said,

> "Tiny stars, if I could catch you,
> To Leilani would I give
> Like her charming string of seashells,
> 'Round a lovely neck you'd live
> You'd adorn her long black tresses
> And be buttons for her dresses
> But she'd glow so bright
> My guess is, less is more...
> The more... that less is?"

Keepsake Box

The box on the facing page was made by Catherine Damon, a young girl bursting with energy. She loves art and drama and is the daughter of Lauren Clark, who made the shell-encrusted box (see page 32). Catherine uses this keepsake box to hold her wonderful treasures. She collected the shells herself and affixed them to the box with Goop.

Sandals with Shells

Sophia Slote, a drama student, is filled with creative enthusiasm, and she has brought that energy to working with shells. The sandals shown below are delightful and will be a lovely addition to any young lady's wardrobe. Sophia's mother, Deborah McDowell, created the shell lampshade (see page 53) and has been a wonderful creative influence on her daughter. The sandals are decorated with shells she collected and applied with hot glue. When Sophia is not romping in her shell-encrusted sandals, she leaves them on her dresser for decoration.

papier-mâché masks covered with shells

Designed by Nicole Monteran

Nicole Monteran was born in France and now lives in Berlin, where she works as a freelance graphic designer and pursues her passions of painting and photography. Nicole has a lively spirit and works in all types of materials. These masks are a wonderful and imaginative project to do with children. They could actually be made at the beach and do not require many tools.

Materials

Plastic bucket

Wallpaper paste

Newspaper

Round head-sized stone

Spoon or stick

Selection of shells

Hair dryer (optional)

Small acrylic paintbrush and acrylic paints (optional)

Sand, stones, and pearl beads (optional)

Household glue (optional)

Staple gun and wire (if hanging the mask)

Hole punch and ribbon (if wearing the mask)

1. In a plastic bucket, mix wallpaper paste and water, following the directions on the label. Soak strips of newspaper in the mixture, then squeeze out the excess moisture from the paper.

Step 2. Applying layers of wet newspaper strips over stone

2. Apply layers of wet newspaper strips over the stone. Build and shape the facial features by applying additional paper. The mask should be 1–1½ inches thick. Apply a layer of paste over the newspaper.

3. While the newspaper is still wet, use a spoon or a stick to scoop out holes for the eyes and the mouth.

4. Push shells into the wet paper. (The shells can be broken up into smaller pieces to create some flat areas on the mask.)

5. Let the mask dry at room temperature for 1 day. To speed the process, use a hair dryer or lay the mask in the sun. When dry, carefully separate the mask from the stone.

6. Decorate the mask further with acrylic paint applied to the newspaper and/or the shells. You can also affix sand, stones, pearl beads, additional shells, and other objects with household glue.

7. With a staple gun, attach wire to the back to hang up the mask. Or punch a hole on each edge and string a ribbon through so the mask can be worn.

Step 4. Pushing shells into wet paper

Shell Holiday Decorations

For a fun, family holiday project, make Christmas tree ornaments from shells collected during a memorable summer vacation. Many shells already have holes worn into them from the surf, but tapping a nail through shells is an easy way to create the holes needed for the wire or string. In some instances, I used a handheld drill to make small holes in shells. The mother-of-pearl buttons, which, of course, already have holes, and a tag sale strand of pearls add to the beach motif shown at left.

Making a shell-encrusted wreath is fairly simple and can be adapted to any wreath material, such as the one made of twigs shown above. I used CG-9000 to affix shells in a balanced design, then tied a ribbon at the bottom.

sands of
TIME

This book began with a discussion of the history of shellwork as an art form, and it seems fitting to conclude with time-honored styles of shellwork that continue today with a contemporary twist. Chief among the traditional forms of shellwork are shell grottoes, pavilions, and rooms. Grottoes, like the one at Woburn Abbey, shown at left, were popular in Europe during the 17th and 18th centuries. They expressed a dark sensibility. In those times, masons did most outdoor shellwork. By contrast, shell rooms inside houses were usually bright, cheerful, and quite feminine, and most of that work was done by women.

> "Shells form a felicitous group, and the sight of them may inspire lofty ideas as to form in architects and sculptors and even in painters."
>
> — Edmé François Gersaint, French trader of choice shells, 1736

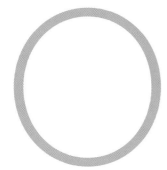riginally natural caves with springs, grottoes were said to be haunted by nymphs. Later, the ancient Greeks and Romans built artificial grottoes as a place for learned discourse. They dedicated them to the Muses, who presided over the arts and the sciences. During the Renaissance, when art focused on imitating — then surpassing — nature, elaborate shell grottoes became a central feature in gardens. Grottoes provided an ideal setting in which artists and architects could experiment with the idea of nature and art's working together toward the perfection of both. They turned to the shell as a decorative material and an inspirational motif.

Rococo, a style of art and architecture that originated in France in the 18th century, was known for its use of fanciful and ornamental shellwork. The term rococo derives from the French word *rocaille,* meaning "loose stones," and is used to refer to a type of rock and shell decoration employed in grottoes. This use of rocaille, in turn, derives from the expression *travail de coquille,* which means shellwork. The shell, by its very shape, was the perfect instrument for the *rocaille* aesthetic of instability and penchant for circular forms and wavy borders.

Following in the tradition of the ancient Greeks and Romans, Alexander Pope began his famous shell grotto in Twickenham, England, around 1720, using it as a place to write and indulge in pleasurable reverie. For Pope, it was a continuous source of inspiration and contentment, a place where the Muses communicated with him, and the origin of many of the pastoral images in his books.

Many of the old European grottoes have been lost to neglect. One such place was the Grotto of Thetis, which Louis XIV built in the park at Versailles in 1665. It had classical architectural features, including a triple doorway and columns with shell capitals, as well as shell chandeliers and fantastic shell masks. Unfortunately, all that remains are some etchings by Jean Le Pautre.

Some grottoes have survived the test of time and are being restored and taken over by Landmark Trusts. For example, the summer residence of Frederick II of Prussia, known as Sanssouci, is located in Potsdam, Germany. The Grotto of Neptune was added to the residence in 1774. It includes an exterior wall encrusted with shells, which is now being restored to its original condition. Listed as a World Heritage Site, the buildings showcase the finest in rococo architecture and landscaping.

The exterior of Sanssouci, shown at top left, has been carefully restored to its former glory. Close-up photos depict Sanssouci's stairway, shown at bottom left. A subterranean shell grotto in Ware, England, was designed by poet John Scott in the early 18th century. The "council chamber," shown above, has 50 shell types and a fringe of barnacles and pearl oysters.

SAND DOLLARS

This poem was written by James Scrimgeour, a professor of English and cochair of the English Department at Western Connecticut State University. He is the author of several books of poems published by Hanover Press.

round shells with a flower design
imprinted on their humped backs,

and the veins in their underbellies,
branching out of the hole that sandpipers

so neatly drill before sucking out
the juiciest flesh morsels, so many,

strewn on the strip of Ocean Beach —
large ones, small ones, dirty ones

clean ones, gray ones, cream ones,
some tinged with black, some with green,

such abundance, you can't pick them all —
your hands, your pockets full —

you're sure you've gathered more
than you'll ever need, or spend . . .

'til settled in your study — 3,000 miles
from the Pacific, you miss the ones

given away, mourn the ones broken
in transit, survey the chips in all

the survivors' edges, and hear the echo
of small white bones — dove wings

fluttering in the vacant shell.

Grottoes are still being constructed all over the world, with a few examples in the United States. In 1973, George Headley transformed a three-car garage into a grotto at La Belle Farm, now part of the Headley–Whitney Museum in Lexington, Kentucky. Headley worked with assistants for nearly a year, gluing shells and polished stones to the walls, doors, and window moldings. He also decorated furnishings with shells, built cabinets to display his fossil and shell collection, and made the floor from coral slabs mined in Key West. Carl Malouf created four shell mosaics depicting exotic sea environments on the ceiling.

Shell Rooms and Pavilions

Shells were also used to make elaborate decorative interiors, and a variety of famous ones survive. Woburn Abbey in Bedfordshire, England, contains the most famous shell room, known as the Grotto. Begun by the fourth Earl of Bedford in 1640, the room took 10 years to complete. It stands at the head of a distinguished series of shell rooms and is considered the forerunner of shell grottoes. Today, the Grotto remains in near perfect condition.

A La Ronde, a 16-sided house completed in 1796 near Exmouth, Devon, is the finest surviving example of interior shellwork practiced by 18th- and 19th-century women. Decorated by Jane and Mary Parminter, the rooms are covered with shell mosaics that alternate with cut paper decorations and bird motifs done in feathers.

Somewhere between outdoor and indoor structures, pavilions were also popular and became a focal point for shellwork. The pavilion at Goodwood Park in West Sussex is noted for the mathematical precision of its interior shellwork. The second Duchess of Richmond and her two daughters spent seven years adorning the walls and domed ceiling to create one of the most elaborate shell rooms in existence. Finished in 1739, it is completely lined with intricate shell mosaic patterns and includes niches with urns filled with shell flowers and shell-framed mirrors.

In France, the Rambouillet Château has a famous shell pavilion built in the second half of the 18th century by the

Duc de Penthièvre for his widowed daughter-in-law. He hoped the cottage, set on a tiny island, would help relieve some of her grief. The thatched roof and rustic exterior give no hint of the sumptuous inlay of shells covering the interior walls. Each wall is composed of eight columns, with each column containing more than 600 shells. Between the columns are pictures made from shells. The mantel has a facade of shells framed by a shell garland.

To outfit these rooms, elaborate furnishings were designed. In the 18th century, Thomas Chippendale devoted a section of his book *Gentleman and Cabinet-Maker's Director* to grotto furniture, which he said contained four basic design forms: scalloped shells, sea horses, dolphins, and triton horns. The furniture was highly decorative — carved and fluted almost to the point of distortion, then finished in lacquered silver leaf. The furnishings, also known as pavilion furniture, were first conceived for George IV's Royal Pavilion in Brighton.

The interior of George Headley's grotto, shown below, is a modern interpretation of an age-old art. The elaborate interior of Sanssouci, shown on pages 134–35, displays an extravagance of shell patterns.

INSPIRATION ON THE OPEN SEA

Another highly decorative traditional art form is sailor's valentines, as these intricate shell mosaics have come to be known. Legend has it that lovesick sailors created them as gifts for their sweethearts during idle hours aboard ships. However, it now appears that a lot of those early works were actually produced in Barbados for the souvenir trade. One thing we can be sure about is that seamen brought them from the Caribbean to New England and then took them across the Atlantic to England. Soon after, Victorian women, enchanted by their romantic lore, took up the art form.

A traditional sailor's valentine is made inside a hinged, usually two-sided wooden box; it is frequently secured with a heart-shaped lock and generally includes an elaborate flower design, a heart shape, and a special verse or message. The Strong Museum in Rochester, New York, houses the largest collection of vintage sailor's valentines, including the one pictured on the facing page. And, of course, these works, imbued with an ancient dreamlike quality, continue to inspire shell artists today.

sailor's valentine

Designed by Sandy Moran

While walking on the beach, Sandy Moran became inspired to create sailor's valentines. She has the skills of a watchmaker, using dental tools to position shells in her intricate, heirloom-quality work. Sandy has received many awards at the Sanibel Shell Fair and shows her pieces in a gallery in Nantucket, Massachusetts, but most of her work comes from commissions. For the center of her designs she uses portraits, miniature Nantucket baskets, and scrimshaw-etched ivory plaques depicting nautical designs. She calls herself a Type A personality because of her attention to detail, and her artwork is intense yet delicate, very much like Sandy herself.

sailor's valentine

Materials

Valentine box

Paper, scissors, ruler, pencil

Tacky glue

Inexpensive paintbrush

Shell dust (see page 93)

Cording or small shells

Bond 527

Tweezers

Shell flowers (see pages 100–101)

Small trinkets, sentimental items, photographs (optional)

1. Select a unique box for your project. It's fun to look for octagonal boxes at antique shows or flea markets. You can find boxes with interesting woods and in all sizes. For a standard box, contact Sanibel Seashell Industry (see Resources on page 150). For your first project, I suggest you start small.

2. Cut a heart template out of paper and place it in the center of the box. Measure from side to side and top to bottom to make sure it is centered. Draw around the outline with a pencil to transfer the shape to the bottom of the box.

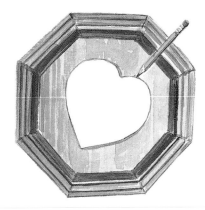

Step 2. Transferring heart pattern to box

3. Mix one-third water to two-thirds tacky glue and apply it with a paintbrush to the area outside the heart. Sprinkle shell dust on this area, but be sure not to cover the pencil line of the heart. Shake out the excess shell dust. This process must be done quickly and accurately. If the shell dust layer is too thin, repeat the process, allowing adequate drying time between coats. Let the box dry overnight.

4. Line the inside edge of the box with cording or small shells. Make a small bead of Bond 527 along the edge, then very carefully place the cording on top of the bead. Or use tweezers to place each shell, one at

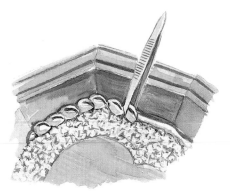

Step 4. Lining inside edge with shells

a time, in the glue. Set them as close as possible along the edge of the box. Let the box dry overnight.

5. Outline the heart with shells using the same method as in step 4. Let it dry overnight.

6. Make enough shell flowers to fill the inside of the heart. Remember — this is *your* valentine, so include whatever you like, such as small trinkets, sentimental items, possibly photographs. Just keep in mind the scale of the item in relation to the entire piece. Arrange the shell flowers, trinkets, and other items inside the heart without using any glue. Reposition them, if you wish.

Step 6. Arranging shells inside heart

7. Once you are satisfied with the composition, take everything out and glue each piece into place using Bond 527. Let it dry overnight. Voilà! Now you have your own sailor's valentine!

THE BONNET HOUSE

Located in Fort Lauderdale, Florida, and nestled on 35 acres along the inter-

coastal waterway, the Bonnet House is a shell lover's paradise. Helen Birch

and Frederic Clay Bartlett, who were given the land as a wedding present,

built the plantation-style house in 1920. In 1930, Frederic Bartlett and his

third wife, Evelyn, built a museum to house her shell collection. The circle-

shaped interior is lined with display shelves, and the walls are covered with a

shell-adorned design. Gigantic clamshells sit on each side of the entrance.

   Both Frederic and Evelyn were accomplished painters, and their cre-

ative energy and sense of whimsy are evident throughout the property.

The grounds display a blend of native and exotic flora and fauna and many

shell-motif elements. Inside the house is an impressive collection of vintage

shell-shaped china; a shell-encrusted arcade

hallway between the dining and the drawing

rooms; shell archways, shown at left; and an

extraordinary display of vintage shell flower

bouquets, such as the one shown at right.

recipes from the shell banquet

Butter-Poached Lobster with Fennel, Pancetta, and Pesto Vinaigrette

Prepared by Bill Webber, owner and chef of Verdura Cucina Rustica, Great Barrington, Massachusetts

Bill is a passionate chef for whom cooking is a sensuous art form. His restaurant is committed to using only the freshest seasonal and organic ingredients and to supporting local farmers and artisans. Bill attended the Culinary Institute of America in Hyde Park, New York, and worked in many fine restaurants before opening Verdura in June 2000. The restaurant's atmosphere and food are strongly inspired by Mediterranean cuisine and lifestyle.

½ cup plus 4 quarts water
4 cups (8 sticks) butter, cubed
3 lobsters
   Salt and freshly ground black pepper
2 bunches fresh basil
1 cup fresh flat parsley leaves
¼ cup pine nuts
1 teaspoon chopped fresh garlic
½ cup grated Parmigiano-Reggiano cheese
1¼ cups plus 2 tablespoons extra virgin olive oil
½ cup rice wine vinegar
¾ cup diced pancetta, rendered
3 artichoke hearts, sliced
2¼ cups shaved fennel
¼ cup fresh lemon juice

1. In a saucepan, bring the ½ cup of water to a boil. Remove the pan from the heat and slowly add the butter in small amounts. Return the pan to low heat, whisking constantly to create an emulsion. After all the butter is incorporated, remove the pan from the heat and reserve it in a warm place on the stove.

2. Lay the lobsters on a towel on top of a cutting board and insert a knife into the back of the head of each one to cut the spinal cord and kill the lobster. Add salt to the 4 quarts of water and bring to a boil over high heat. Remove the tails and claws and place them in the boiling water for 4 minutes. Use tongs to remove them from the pot and place them in an ice bath to cool. When they are cool, remove the shells and reserve the meat.

3. Set aside several basil leaves to use as garnish. Place the remaining basil, parsley, pine nuts, and garlic in a food processor and blend until fine. Stop the processor and add the cheese, a pinch of salt, and a pinch of pepper. Start the machine again and, as it is running, incorporate ¼ cup of the olive oil to make a pesto.

4. Place 2 tablespoons of the pesto in a bowl with the rice wine vinegar and whisk vigorously. As you whisk, slowly incorporate 1 cup more of the olive oil. Season the dressing with salt and pepper.

5. Cut the lobster tails in half lengthwise and clean out the intestinal tract with water. Place all of the lobster meat, including the claws, in the reserved butter sauce and poach the pieces for 4 minutes.

6. Heat a skillet with the remaining 2 tablespoons of olive oil and add the pancetta, artichokes, and fennel. Heat them until they are warm and add the lemon juice and salt and pepper to taste. Place piles of warm salad in the center of six plates, remove the lobster from the butter, and top each plate with one claw and half a tail. Spoon the pesto vinaigrette over and around the salads and garnish them with the reserved basil leaves.

Yield: 6 servings

Recommended Reading

Dance, S. Peter. *DK Handbooks: Shells.*
London: DK Publishing, 2000.
Krauss, Helen. *Shell Art: A Handbook for
Making Shell Flowers, Mosaics, Jewelry, and
Other Ornaments.* New York: Dover
Publications, 1976.
Mauriés, Patrick. *Shell Shock:
Conchological Curiosities.* New York:
Thames and Hudson, 1994.
Ritchie, Carson I. A. *Shell Carving:
History and Techniques.* South
Brunswick, N.J.: A. S. Barnes, 1974.
Smyth, Carole, and Richard Smyth.
Neptune's Treasures. Huntington, N.Y.:
Carole Smyth Antiques, 1988.

Resources

SHELLS

Sanibel Seashell Industries
239-472-1603
www.seashells.com

Sea Shell City, Inc.
888-743-5524
www.seashellcity.com

She Sells Sea Shells
239-472-6991
www.sanibelshellcrafts.com
Shell crafts are sold online, but individual
shells are sold only at their retail stores

Shell Factory and Nature Park
800-282-5805
www.shellfactory.com

Shell Horizons Inc.
727-536-3333
www.shellhorizons.com

Shells by Emily
239-394-5575
www.shellsbyemily.com

GLUE

FPC Corporation
800-860-3838
www.surebonder.com
Manufacturer of Surebonder glues and
supplies

MARBLEIZED PAPER

Paper Mojo
800-420-3818
www.papermojo.com

MOTHER-OF-PEARL BUTTONS

Renaissance/Blue Moon Buttons
866-692-3252
www.renaissancebuttons.com

Trims & Buttons, Inc.
213-689-9110
www.buttons4u.com

MISCELLANEOUS

Creel and Gow
(formerly Ruzzetti & Gow)
www.creelandgow.com

Currey & Company
877-768-6428
www.curreycodealers.com

Cyber Island Shops Inc.
Orlando, Florida
888-974-3557
www.cyberislandshops.com
Retail only

Elegant Cheese Cakes
650-728-2248
www.elegantcheesecakes.com

Mullin-Jones Antiquities
Great Barrington, Massachusetts
413-528-4871
Retail only

Contributing Artists

*The following information listed for the
contributors was accurate as of the first
printing of this book (2002).*

Lauren Clark
P.O. Box 372
Housatonic, MA 01236
lcncate@bcn.net

Scott Clark
P.O. Box 258
Housatonic, MA 01236
wsc111@hotmail.com

Janet Cooper
P.O. Box 37
Sheffield, MA 01257
Tinjanet@aol.com

Michael Doherty
28 Fruit Street
Northampton, MA 01060
QDOTSYX@cs.com

Anne Fredricks
77 Seekonk Cross
Great Barrington, MA 01230
www.annefredricks.com

Ann Getsinger
P.O. Box 207
Mill River, MA 01244

Goz Gosselin
Fine Shell Art
16279 Charleston Avenue
Fort Myers, FL 33908
860-379-3871 (summer)
239-466-1594 (winter)
terriandgoz@prodigy.net

Robin Greeson
Textile Restoration
P.O. Box 313
East Alford Road
West Stockbridge, MA 01266

Pamela Hardcastle
Garden & Floral Design
Route 57
New Marlborough, MA 01230
prh@zenn.net

Susie Hardcastle
P.O. Box 95
East Hill Road
Southfield, MA 01259
www.pamelahardcastle.com

Mimi Krysiak
P.O. Box 598
Sheffield, MA 01257

Reginald Madison
1699 North Main Street
Sheffield, MA 01257

Marlene Marshall
P.O. Box 363
Sheffield, MA 01257
marleneveronica@hotmail.com
www.mosaicsmarlene.com

Deborah McDowell
Club & Cafe Helsinki
Great Barrington, MA 01230
clubhelsinki@taconic.net

Nicole Monteran
Roennester 7
D14057 Berlin, Germany
n.moneran@gmx.de

Sandy Moran
Sailor's Valentine Studio
P.O. Box 629
Yarmouth Port, MA 02675
508-362-8410 (summer)
941-472-7705 (winter)
seashells5@earthlink.net
www.sailorsvalentinestudio.com

Dana and Fritz Rohn
Jennings and Rohn Antiques
530 Milton Road
Litchfield, CT 05759
drohn@snet.net

Ron Ronan
Elements
Great Barrington, MA 01230
jill@elementsjillswartz.com

William Schade
199 The Knolls
Williamstown, MA 01267

Jim Scrimgeour
36 Caldwell Streeet
New Milford, CT 06776
SCRIMGEOUR@wcsub.ctstateu.edu

Janice Shields
326 Old Sturbridge Road
Lenox, MA 01240

Robin Smiddtt
Tokonoma Gallery & Framing Studio
P.O. Box 519, 405 Park Street
Housatonic, MA 01236
413-274-1166

Sabine Vollmer von Falken
P.O. Box 109
Glendale, MA 01229
www.svfphotoart.com

Bill Webber
Verdura Cucina Rustica
44 Railroad Street
Great Barrington, MA 01230
413-528-8969

Eve Zatt
P.O. Box 134
Spencertown, NY 12165
elzatt@hotmail.com

Photo Credits

An old mirror gets new life with delicate shell flowers designed by Goz Gosselin.

index